JEREMIAH J. BROWN

BANK ON YOU

You don't need an advisor; you need a financial education overhaul.

WHAT CAN I TEACH YOU
ABOUT MONEY!?

Why should anyone listen to me?

I've asked myself this question many times. Through examining the decision of whether or not I am the right person to share financial knowledge, I decided to conduct research on the number of millionaires in the world who obtained their wealth through inheritance, and what the qualifications are for being considered "self-made." After all, what differentiates me from someone who's successfully accomplished the task of accumulating massive amounts of wealth starting from ZERO!?

Well, here is what I found:

- 2/3 of people who accumulated massive amounts of wealth actually inherited it. Yes, that is 66% of total millionaires and billionaires in existence! This leaves us with 1/3 of the wealthy population who are considered self-made, which is still not terrible.

- Criteria of being self-made: become rich by own efforts or *increase the amount acquired through inheritance by 2 times or more (case in point, Donald Trump)*.

The reality and beauty of learning is you don't need to learn how to drive from a professional race car driver in order to excel at driving. In many cases, you can learn how to drive from someone who's gone through a similar process and who can relate and understand where you've been and where you're going. The same rules apply in learning about money, how it works, and how to build wealth. Financial literacy is not a skill, people; it's a lifestyle!

So, why not me?!

RESULTS OF POPULAR FINANCIAL (Rhetoric) ADVICE:

*"Close to 30% of households 55 and over have
NO retirement savings or pension."*

—Smart Assets

"62% of Americans have less than $1,000 saved for an emergency."

—Market Watch

"Nearly 9/10 people worldwide are NOT happy with their jobs."

—Forbes

"157 million Americans have credit card debt to pay off."

—CNBC

"1 in 3 Americans have nothing saved for retirement."

—E*TRADE

"Americans hold over $1 trillion in credit card debt."

—Federal Reserve

"44 million have student loan debt OUTSTANDING."

—CNBC

"8/10 Americans LIVE in debt."

—CNBC

PREFACE

It is 7:30 a.m., L.A. time.

I am driving apprehensively through skid row as I race to my morning meeting in downtown, Los Angeles, with an angel investor to pitch a technology product that I developed. Sprinting through yellow lights and struggling to get to my destination on time, I awkwardly came to a quick break at a red light. Looking to my left out of the driver's side window, I noticed a homeless woman approaching, asking for change. I politely rolled down my window and gave her a few bucks. By this time the light turned green, indicating the continuation of my current destination. I rolled up my window and continued my commute. But as she began to fade into my rearview, something dawned on me . . .

Did she have any debt?

I always wondered why society often frowns upon the homeless. We look at a homeless and economically deprived person, and subconsciously analyze and judge their socioeconomic status; no job, no income, no debt. Wait, no debt!? Yes, that is correct, the average homeless person has NO DEBT. But why is this so significant? After all, even with our five- or six-figure debt load, there is income coming in to supplement it, right!?

(Photo: Alexia Lex, Getty Images/iStockphoto)

*The average American household has over 15K in credit card debt and over 130K in total debt and growing!

The reality is, we live in an illusion of wealth, while the homeless live in the reality of their financial situation. If you understand how our monetary system works (if you don't, read my book *Financial Freedom: My Only Hope*), then you know debt is an intrinsic part of our economy and is the steam that keeps this economic train moving. But here is what worries me regarding homeless people reflecting financial reality. If there is interest due on every dollar in existence, what happens to our system if the fed curtails or completely stops its fiat currency printing? It is actually quite simple; we would probably have to move into the tent next door. Since there is payment due every month on every dollar ever created, along with new currency replacing old currency (which creates inflation), stopping the creation of new dollars in order to pay for old dollars will cause a deflationary event and collapse the entire economy. This means that our monetary system is designed to require everlasting debt creation just to continue! With this universal law regarding how money works, which is embedded within the fabric of our system, how is it that we rely on contrary financial advice such as saving, paying down debt, and submitting our money to financial experts who will utilize this universal law of *leverage*, in hopes of producing high and even infinite returns on our money? What if I told you that, even with all of the antiquated financial information and advice given to you by top-tier financial experts and economists, they are not responsible for this economic disparity. We are.

We know that something is terribly wrong within our economy and financial systems. We question the massive printing of fiat currency, the digital printing of the fractional reserve system, rising prices of everyday goods and services and even the astronomical cost of our basic necessities—food, education, shelter, etc. Yet, there is one catalyst that we avoid questioning in the first place. Whether because of our sheer ignorance, indoctrination, or acquiescing to the economic mechanism at hand, we never ask why do we have to pay to be alive to begin with? Unfortunately, once something is engrained into society's thinking and way of life, it's almost impossible to reevaluate antiquated methodologies such as trading paper for real value, and to reimagine what a *fair* economy looks like. Oddly enough, we are obliviously participating and living in this people farm that is managed by the system of debt slavery, whereby all the inhabitants are forced to strip-mine the earth around them in order to collect the paper they need to pay to be alive. But, at what cost? I don't think any solution and financial advice is that simple. However, if you're going to participate in this game and wonder how to build more wealth, then the solution will be simpler than answering this question.

In this book, I intend not only to debunk the over-the-counter mainstream financial information and advice frequently handed to the masses, but offer real-world solutions for beating this game of financial chess, even on a shoestring budget. If you are interested in producing an infinite return starting from a place of zero, or wherever you currently are financially, then read further. It will shift your perspective about the financial information normally given and allow you to start amassing wealth like the wealthy. Let us begin!

CONTENTS

INTRODUCTION   xv

Chapter 1
EQUITY IS THE HOLY GRAIL   1

Chapter 2
WEALTH TRAPS EXPOSED AS GOOD ADVICE   19

Chapter 3
THE FUTURE OF INVESTING   37

Chapter 4
BLOCKCHAIN: THE NEW FREE MARKET?   59

Chapter 5
PROTECT YOUR CASTLE: CORPORATIONS   71

Chapter 6
THE CREDIT HACK   81

Chapter 7
GoFundMe IS NOT LIFE INSURANCE   95

Chapter 8
ALL BUSINESS   103

Chapter 9
PROFIT LIKE A BIG WIG   115

Chapter 10
HOW MUCH DOES A DOLLAR COST?   131

INTRODUCTION

The key to financial freedom is to use an investment that grows your INCOME, not your savings.

The cosmic irony puzzles me!

There are countless of financial professionals and experts, combined with a sea of financial resources available; however, the income gap and wealth disparity continue to climb to the highest levels not seen since the Great Depression. It's almost as if there is a more intrinsic factor plaguing people from achieving financial success. Are higher forces or the powers that be amassing wealth at our expense (pun intended)? Possibly. However, I believe there is an insidious, stealth engine spearheading this—the engine of too much of the same financial information being offered by our mainstream media. Things like:

- *Slash your credit cards*

- *Max out your 401k*

- *Hand your money over to a financial expert*

- *Look the part (wear your money on your sleeve, literally)*

- *Your house is an asset*

- *Student loans are good debt*

- *blah blah blah . . .*

Financial Fast Food

The reality is, when it comes to advice about improving our finances, we are actually drowning in a sea of information! However, all of the information seems to be backed mostly by rhetoric and popular consensus of practices of wealth building. It is almost as if the only solution to becoming wealthy outside of the obvious (entertainer, athlete, actor, etc.) is to retire your money and wait until you're old and wrinkled to recoup your investment. I believe this is mediocre financial information, or what I refer to as financial fast food. Living well below your means, blindly trusting your money to the markets, and hopelessly waiting until you're old to become a millionaire sounds more like a financial uncertainty than plausible advice. This kind of cheap and convenient mass information is exclusively for the masses, similar to McDonald's. The difference is the box of goods we're sold is for financial education instead of cheap, questionably nutritious food. The result? Take a look around you. There is that MBA graduate still living at home with his parents, that Uber driver who is balancing two jobs and still needs another gig in order to stay afloat. That 60-something year old who has to continue to work even when she should've retired a long time ago. These are the consequences of following the ubiquitous and antiquated financial advice in our new economic world.

If there is a ton of accurate financial information out there, then why is close to 80% of the population living paycheck to paycheck? And why is it that although the average U.S. salary is $68,000, more than half of the people have less than $1,000 in total savings (57%)? The real question isn't, Why don't we have information available about how to care for our personal finances? Rather, we need to question, is this the right information being given to us? If the information given to us is correct and easily available, why are we not motivated to do what we know we should be doing? Yes, I am challenging us. From the highest income earners, to the average person on a modest salary. Even the person with too much month at the end of their money, or no income at all.

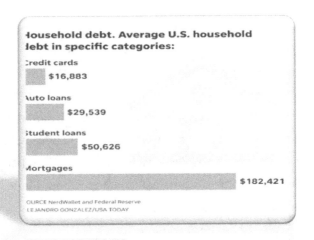

Household debt. Average U.S. household debt in specific categories:

Credit cards
$16,883

Auto loans
$29,539

Student loans
$50,626

Mortgages
$182,421

SOURCE NerdWallet and Federal Reserve
LEJANDRO GONZALEZ/USA TODAY

Of course, there is no single answer for this. Most people are not motivated to save money or invest, but to spend it on emulating the lifestyles of the people they admire, whether this means eating at the same restaurants, wearing the same clothes, or driving the same cars as their idols and influencers. Advertisement companies, along with the media, play a huge role in this irrational form of consumerism. From determining the latest trends, to glorifying how the rich live and spend their money, it almost seems as if people are being robbed of the motivation to do things the right way, simply because of the financial distraction to stay current and keep up with the Joneses. Don't believe me? Allow me to ask you the following questions:

1. Do you feel as if you must have the latest smartphone, the latest 50-inch television, or a luxury car with built-in Wi-Fi connectivity?

2. When a person moves into a house with an outdated kitchen (let's say from the 1980s), is the key motivation to update it (because today granite countertops are the new standard)?

Whether or not you are convinced by these sample impulse-related questions representing our inundation in the world of mass consumerism, I am sure you understand where I am going here. The beliefs that have been subconsciously engrained in our minds create a never-ending cycle of consumerism. If you want to beat this financial deception and achieve real wealth, then it is imperative that you learn something fundamentally different about money. Remember, you can't change your financial situation living by the same information you had before opening this book.

The shocking truth

I find it extraordinary when people have their first liquidity event and obtain capital, whether through a tax refund, income from a sale of company or property, signing a major contract, suit, receiving an advance, or through receiving inheritance money, and they blow it all on pure consumption to look rich and invest in things that financial experts deem an asset. The truth is, if we don't come clean about the abundant financial rhetoric out there (which, statistically proven, is not working for the majority) and come up with real-world solutions to help us create infinite returns and build wealth (even with a small budget), then I'm afraid the wealth and income disparity that we see in the world will only rise. This is where I come in. Whether through sharing my personal experience or what I've learned through the mentorship of millionaires, I will reveal the financial knowledge that can help you go from zero to infinite, especially with your investment returns. So, without further ado, let's get right into . . .

What Is an *Infinite Return?*

- *When your **principal** is no longer **included** with your investment*

- *When you are able to produce cash flow **FOREVER***

- *When you can **mass-produce** and **scale** a product or service with little to no money invested*

- *When your money starts **working** for you*

Are you ready to start producing infinite returns?

Please continue →

CHAPTER 1

EQUITY IS THE HOLY GRAIL

Is patrimonial the new capitalism?

We are going to get right into it!

What I am about to reveal may be viewed by some as a financial watershed moment. The kind of esoteric information that could explode like a supernova in the brain. Nearly six centuries after Johannes Gutenberg devised the first printing press, it's still possible for a subtle nuance such as ink on a page to shake the very foundation, disrupt antiquated philosophies, unravel ideologies, and arm people with the knowledge needed to combat insidious powers that have robbed them of the ability to achieve economic freedom and prosperity on this planet. What I am referring to is a future governed and dominated by inherited wealth. This is the future of *patrimonial capitalism.*

> ### 2/3 of ALL wealth is intergenerational.
> —CNBC study

High (R), Low (G), bad for our economy

The rise of patrimonial capitalism has forced capital to be concentrated in the hands of the few, giving these specific groups of people power over political, economic, and social rule, disrupting the very fabric of our so-called democracy. Between the years of 1971 and 2016, more than 60% of our nation's income went to the richest 1% of the population. This is something no industry pundits, financial experts, or media wants to take into consideration, as they provide us with antiquated and ineffectual financial advice. I believe that revealing this reality would, in fact, change the way we approach personal finance and possibly even economics as it relates to our monetary system. Sure, the conversation of income and wealth inequality has been in the forefront of our society for a long time now. However, there is no conversation focusing on whether or not popular and commercialized financial advice actually works. The world is now moving in a direction not favorable to the economically deprived or financially incompetent. Normally characterized as the income and wealth gap, these inequalities are moving beyond a finite point in time. These inequalities are now becoming transferred from generation to generation.

This is because the rate of economic growth tends to trail the rate of return on capital.

➤ *Average return on **CAPITAL**: 5% to 7%*

➤ *Average growth rate of the **ECONOMY**: 2% to 3%*

*When you have a **high *rate of return on capital*** and **a low *growth rate in the economy***, you have the ingredients of an *oligarchy*.

What this means is that, on average, families within the 1% and .01%, who have amassed a fortune through inheritance, will have enough money to live an abundant life, and still set aside money that will always outpace the growth rate of the overall economy. When you have a situation where an inheritor can maintain a certain life-style with his inheritance, and still have stashed capital outpacing the economy, this will always lead to a wealth and income divide in America.

Why do we care?

So, who cares if capital outpaces our economy, and that the rich, including those inheriting massive fortunes, are benefiting from this economic advantage? You're probably saying, "Why should I care? I am making my money. I shouldn't be bothered with counting someone else's pocket, right?" Well, allow me to explain. Two words: Political control. Allow me to introduce you to Donald Trump. He is the poster child of buying one's way into the political system, and why we should care. Unfortunately, he is just a diminutive speck in an ever-flowing ocean of the wealthy individuals buying our political system, and who have this system serving their own interests. Doing this reinforces the concentration of income and wealth to the very few, at the expense of the many.

By the year 2030, the 1% will own 2/3 of the entire world's wealth.

—Business Insider

If you have a conversation with an ordinary person about what real wealth looks like in our country, she will have probably have no real clue. She may say things like "having a million dollars makes you wealthy," or "a high-paying job earning six figures makes you wealthy." She will point to an athlete earning a ton of cash or to an entertainer's net worth as a representation of what wealth looks like. However, the tremendous size of the fortunes of the people who own real wealth are so far out of the scope of the average person's mind that it almost seems impossible and elusive to fully understand. Most people have no idea how far the economic divide is between their favorite celebrity and the elite and wealthy .01%, let alone the average American!

➤ *Average American's net worth: $68,000*

➤ *Founder of Amazon's net worth: $100,000,000,000*

A dirty, but necessary word

America's historical claims to being a democratic society are now being threatened by this inequality of wealth that surpasses the average person's understanding. Tax breaks, low interest rates, and tax havens have throughout history been a form of corporate welfare. There are many studies pointing to taxes and inflation as insidiously and covertly redistributing wealth from the hands of the many to the very few.

> *90% of the tax code is written to bene-*
> *fit entrepreneurs and investors.*

—Provision Wealth

There has been a whining from the wealthy about this topic for decades now. So much so, that they designed an insidious and effective apparatus embedded within the media and mainstream sources of financial information that silences any noise against the case of a redistribution of wealth. The irony is, the redistribution of wealth is often now viewed as averse to the democratic principles of our society, and a threat to patriotism. On the contrary, if you look at American history, this position is not at all true. From the beginning of the United States as a free and independent nation, a fair distribution of wealth had been raised as an ideal worth fighting for.

So, what is the solution? Well, if we, instead of taxing the wealthy, aggregate a mandatory *innovation fund* from the .01%, taking from the elite few a percent of national income, funneling it through a fund directed to the bottom 20%, we could finance many important things that affect the standards of wealth and well-being for the many, such as access to essential, basic healthcare and innovations that tap into accessing the entrepreneurial creativity of the poor and disenfranchised, who have a will and ideas for creating and growing wealth but lack the means to begin.

The .01% could even have a vested interest in this fund as it increases in gains from the returns of innovation, similar to a venture capital structure, which would definitely entice the wealthy to partake in this (secret tax). This would also allow them to relinquish the negative stigma of the greedy capitalist and instead be portrayed as capitalists with hearts (we would still need heavy PR for this).

The reality is, until we can come clean about what is really creating this economic divide, then this antiquated form of financial rhetoric, disguised as great advice, will continue to appropriate mainstream financial education, which leads to an abysmal global income and wealth disparity.

You cannot reason with a tiger, when your head is in its mouth.

—Winston Churchill

If you can't beat em', join em'

Realistically speaking, if all we are going to do about this situation is talk, then the issue will never be solved completely. There are many solutions that could possibly help even the score and close the enormous wealth and income gaps within our countries. However, I come from the school of results. My solution? Follow the model!

There is a reason why you should stress creating a legacy for your children. The solution, although a pragmatic one, is still a hard economic journey to endure. I mean, you are working, saving, and investing not only for your future, but for the future that will follow, even after you no longer exist. It's almost poetic in theory and financially bittersweet. I mean why would anyone rely on blind faith and take the chance to build wealth only to pass it down later on for someone else to enjoy? Even deeper, how can you trust the next generation will honor your gift, replicate the model, and continue to pay it forward? This answer is heavily reliant on your ability to understand three basic steps in building generational wealth.

These steps consist of the following:

1. **Owning your income** – *Owning your income simply means, owning an asset that will provide cash flow for you. This owned income is normally derived from a cash-producing asset that you own. By owning your income, you have the ability to pass this ownership down to your offspring and heirs. The income from your labor should in fact be one of your many different categories of creating wealth.*

2. **Teaching the model early** – *After you've created multiple streams of income, along with asset acquisition, educate the next generation on how to preserve that income. Don't be afraid to show them how the process works, your income from it, the cost and maintenance expenses associated, and even the taxes you pay on these income streams. This will give them a better understanding of how money works, and how to not only maintain the income, but also master it. The earlier they are able to learn from you, the more likely it will be that they will master the preservation strategy.*

3. **Legally granting ownership** – *Refrain from being the person who, God forbids, passes on and has your assets go into probate for family members and strangers to battle over. There are many ways to ensure that after you pass, your assets are protected for your loved ones. Whether you decide to set up wills, trusts, or transfer ownership to your loved ones, legally granting ownership will ensure that your legacy is protected. This strategy of legal protection is a subtle but critical one, which will help prevent any financial heartache for your family and loved ones, after you are long gone.*

With the help of these simple and pragmatic solutions, you would drastically decrease the failure rate of inheritance as it is passed down from one generation to another. It is extremely critical that you get this right, because without the power of passing down wealth, I am afraid that you will be at the mercy of the 1-percenters controlling the 40+% of the nation's wealth. Ownership is an essential remedy to set yourself financially free and to pass this economic independence down to the next generation.

Cash is no longer king – Equity is

"Cash is king!" says the old and misinformed financial advisors.

Well, to their credit, once upon a time cash *WAS* king. But one summer afternoon, on August, 15, 1971, cash was dethroned by legislation. Its successor? *Cash flow*! Sure, there was a time when this antiquated financial advice of saving cash, living off of the interest of the money saved, and continuing to work hard to accumulate more cash, applied to wealth and retirement planning. But in this new regime of money, our currency is no longer money. Today, equity has become the holy grail.

The economy behind the currency

Presently, working hard for fiat money without converting it into an economic asset is financial suicide! It is the equivalent to holding your breath under water. You may be fine for a while, but eventually, you will run out of air. Unfortunately, these types of currencies, by design, are almost destined to collapse. This is because the fiat currency is debt based and created out of thin air.

The inevitable collapse of the value of fiat currency has been proven throughout the history of our monetary existence dating back to the continental dollar. Fiat currency has been replaced many times and will probably continue. What does not collapse, however, are the mechanisms of the economy behind the currency. Certain aspects of any economy are unchanged, regardless if there is a Great Depression, a Great Recession, and so on. These are the everyday and ubiquitous things that people need in order to live. Procter & Gamble is a company that owns everyday goods, services, and appliances that we use, even during difficult financial times, such as the recent recession. Assets that provide housing, food, transportation, or even education will always be in demand. Just find the assets you think are recession-proof and return cash back to you and invest. This is how you protect yourself.

Want to be financially free?

The true goal of financial freedom is not to make enough money to buy any object that you want. Instead, the goal of financial freedom is to make money *NEVER* be an object! It's a subtle, but huge distinction. If pursuing multiple streams of income, acquiring assets that pay you, being your own boss, or even having the freedom to make your own schedule sounds daunting and unrealistic to you, then you must simply alter how you think. Ultimately, if you are interested in pursuing financial freedom, you must first change your mind-set. Let's take a look at the mind-set of the poor, middle class (if there still is one), and the rich in terms of how they approach money.

Poor:

Focus *only* on trying to pay their bills. Likely live paycheck to paycheck.

Middle class:

Focus on buying stuff in order to appear rich, but sink deeper and deeper in consumer (bad debt) debt. If they do invest, they turn over their money to a financial manager, and retire their money by placing it into mutual funds, 401k, or the house that they own.

The wealthy:

Focus on the *velocity of money*, leveraging their money or (other people's money) into an asset, and moving their money out of the asset, letting the asset produce cash flow for them. They then rinse and repeat. The wealth investor focuses on acquiring assets and letting the cash flow pay for any of their liabilities. They work because they want to!

Please note that although this is a great blueprint to follow, the learning curve is often very steep and extremely painful. In the beginning, the process may require a ton of initial effort and failure. I advise that you start small, especially if you are starting with little or no resources. This will help you mitigate your risk and increase your acumen and financial knowledge exponentially. You will see that when you *shift your focus* from making piles of money, to making streams of money, you will begin to see the change in your mind-set. But always remember, if you don't put your money to work, if you don't hire your money, your money will hire you to work hard for it.

What is your personal EQUITY?

In order to get a better idea of what a company's balance sheet looks like, I often encourage people to sit down and try to determine their own equity on a balance sheet. Are you willing to try this exercise? Let's do it!

Write down all of your ASSETS here:

1. *Cash (in your bank):*

    _____

2. *Car's current worth* (not what you bought it for*):*

    _____

3. How much is *your house worth?*

    _____

4. List and price *all other assets (anything that pays you):*

    _____, _____,

    _____, _____.

Write down all of your ***LIABILITIES*** here:

1. *Credit card debt:*

    _____

2. *Your home's mortgage:*

    _____

3. *Car note:*

_____

4. List and price all *other liabilities (anything that costs you money):*

_____, _____,

_____, _____.

Next: Add up all of your assets, then subtract them from your liabilities:

Total assets: _____

(minus)

Total liabilities: _____

This should give you your personal *EQUITY* or **NET WORTH:** _____

This will shed a whole lot of light on your real financial situation. You might be earning six or even seven figure incomes a year; however, the only thing you're worth on the books is your personal equity or your *net worth.* The good news is, doing this simple exercise first-hand is the most simplistic way of taking control of your future and understanding your margin of safety.

Congratulations! You now know Margin of Safety.

Would you like to know something great? By participating in the previous exercise, you now have the power to analyze a business and determine the riskiness of the business, just like Warren Buffett. Warren Buffett's criteria for determining the risk factor of a business is margin of safety. If a business doesn't have a substantial amount of safety between what the market price is and what the actual equity is, Buffett is extremely hesitant to move forward with buying the business.

The risk between what you buy the company for and its equity is called the *margin of safety*. The closer the equity is to the market price, the safer the investment. For example, let's say that you are interested in buying a dry cleaning business, and want to know if the sale price justifies the success of the business, or if it would be a good investment. What most people normally do is buy the business just because of how much revenue the business or company produces. However, revenue is not a good indicator of how good an investment it is. The net equity compared to the debt is! This is because anything can go wrong with the business, from an important employee quitting, to a loss in customers due to a competitor entering the space next door, that will cause revenue to drop. The real indicator that will save you from financial ruin is the equity that is in the company, its book value. If you are not analyzing this important component, you will not know if you're getting screwed in the deal or not. And as the saying goes, "If you don't know who the idiot in the deal is, then, most likely, it is you!"

If you're interested in buying a business similar to the following types of businesses, first calculate the margin of safety:

- *Laundromat*

- *Gas station*

- *Restaurant*

- *Trucking company*

- *Senior care – assisted living*

- *Marijuana dispensary*

- *Franchise*

- *Liquor stores*

- *Nail & beauty shop*

- *Car wash*

- *Self storage unit*

- _____ *(your business)*

By evaluating the equity of the business like you did for your personal equity, along with figuring out the margin of safety, you will have used a very simple but effective tool to determine the value of the business. Margin of safety is one of the safest parameters used by the wealthy to buy undervalued businesses. You can apply the same method to evaluate and mitigate the risk of owning any business you are considering.

Follow the money

Most people have a vision of building a market on wheels, serving convenience and traditional food quick and easy, such as burgers and fries. Two dynamic businesswomen, the founders of Baby's Badass Burgers, turned this vision into a reality. Although they were able to build a business attractive enough to appear on the largest national venture capital show in the U.S., *Shark Tank*, they made a classic mistake. They were sharp, articulate, and well versed in presenting, but failed to follow a fundamental tenet of business—follow the money! Now, I know what you're probably thinking; shouldn't they have followed their passion instead, and in return the money would come? Right, as if the market gives a shit! In any business, it's better to follow the green then a dream. In fact, it's your dream of providing value that will lead you to the green. Either way, in any business, it's the green that you should be pursuing.

There is a difference between chasing and following the money.

—Anonymous

This was a very important lesson on maximizing value and sticking to the rivers and the lakes that you're used to (*shameless TLC plug*). They had a working concept—a profitable food trucking business. Instead of requesting capital from the sharks to replicate the trucks, they decided to seek capital to open a brick-and-mortar business. This was a damaging and exorbitant strategy, because operating a physical location would cost 10 times the amount that they were looking for. Producing food trucks, on the contrary, would yield 10 times the leverage, 10 times the sales, with the same amount of money invested. Which would you choose?

Instead of considering making more trucks, which was extremely profitable, they asked for 250k (30% of their company) to totally abandon their cash cow. They eventually failed to get a deal, but left with much valuable information. Sometimes we look towards the dream and forget what we have in front of us. The same rules apply in any business endeavor. If the model is working, why reinvent the wheel? In most cases, innovation is key, but only if it coincides with the universal tenet of following the money. In the growth phase, there is such a thing as pivoting. However, you only pivot to get to a revenue model that will no longer allow you to pivot. The key is to identify what is working and ramp up on that. Ultimately, you must stick to this universal business principle if you want to own a consistent one.

The jobs of the future will be created by YOU?

There are a ton of valid concerns these days, one of which is that the emergence of technology and automation has put us on a definitive path of a jobless future. A recent study from Forrester Research showed that close to 25 million jobs will disappear within the next 10 years, more than 3 times the amount of jobs lost after the financial crisis in 2008. As machines continue to evolve and learn more technical and flexible skills, eventually technology can replace the workload of the smartest and brightest in the sectors requiring highly educated and expertly skilled employees in the white-collar space, placing qualified and high-income earners at risk of this technological revolution. Why is this the case? Why is it that, even as we witness this revolution coming, we are not acting on this outcome sooner? We could point to the fact that modern society continues to be educated through an antiquated educational system, or that we are still holding onto this industrial-like mind-set of an economy and work world soon extinct, the mind-set that trains us to be humanized robots on an assembly line and process the same work and information daily with no adaptation to innovation. However, if we don't fix this problem soon, or adapt to this new environment, we could be staring at a future of ever rising unemployment, homelessness, and financial ruin.

> *What you choose to work on and who you choose to work with, are far more important than how hard you work.*
>
> —Naval Ravikant

In the age of technology and robotics, which have created the obsolescence of our old industry, the key to combating this economic and job-killing plague is to redefine what work looks like, and to create a new program of education that unlocks the hidden talents and passions that we live with each and every day. In the future, I think it is safe to say that the idea of a successful career will not look like the ones advertised in the past. Gone are the days of the suited man or woman working from a corner office suite, or of a proven veteran who has to work for x amount of years in order to share experience-obtained knowledge and expertise. Today, we are witnessing the age of a technology and social media revolution in how we define success, along with the growth rate of it. The future of job creation will come from, dare I say it, collaboration, social media, and technology. Many of the traditional methods of finding opportunities have become irrelevant, being replaced instead by technology.

CHAPTER 2

WEALTH TRAPS EXPOSED AS GOOD ADVICE

Interestingly enough, low income is not always to blame for financial hardship. According to debt.com, only 1 in 5 people (20%) facing financial hardship fall below the poverty line and make less than $40,000 per year. The remaining groups consist of ordinary wage earners and high-income earners who all fit the same spending and debt predicament. I am pretty sure you know a person earning a ton of money who still struggles financially. I know quite a few. I bring this up because with a fleeting middle class, and 80% of the population carrying some form of personal debt, it is quite obvious that we all have been plagued by financial illiteracy, consumerism, and wealth traps. Just because a person makes big bucks, doesn't mean she has a high financial IQ. Having a high financial IQ means knowing how to *control* money and make it work for you. Controlling it does not have to mean cutting back on your expenses, or paying down debt, which is the rhetoric we commonly and repeatedly hear through the media and financial advice industry.

Wealth trap #1
"A penny saved is a penny earned."

A great quote that sounds powerful coming from many of your favorite financial experts, right? Believe this and you will never achieve financial freedom. A penny saved is just that; a penny. Once inflation is done with that penny, you will need another penny just to equal the value of the one you had before! Saving in itself is not bad, but the masses are so focused on saving they never expand their money. No one ever got rich simply by saving money; they just got old.

In order to remedy this, you have to focus on the speed of money as opposed to the security of it. Money moves at a pace that rivals hyperinflation. So as the prices of everyday goods and services rise, your money has to rise just as fast in order to survive in this economic environment. In the end, you should focus on the velocity of your money, leveraging capital to produce an asset that pays you cash flow. The notion of saving just to save is an antiquated one, taken from the old testament of financial advice. Today, if you are ever given the financial strategy to save, your reply should always be, "Sure, then what?" Asking this simple question will train your mind to see the big picture of how money works and put you on the right track to have your money beat inflation along with the economic growth rate.

Wealth trap #2
"Playing a financial game you don't understand"

I can admit, I am a huge *Mad Money* fan, a show on CNBC designed to teach and offer financial information about the stock market in a fanatical way. I frequently tune in. Based on the ratings, it amazes me how we are so reliant on the advice of popular financial gurus on the big screen and industry advisors, that we listen to someone telling us just to invest in different index and mutual funds, and make speculative investments. They may tell us to do our "homework" before making an "investment." However, I highly doubt a single mom raising two or more kids, a man working two different jobs, a person who has never studied money, or even a celebrity who is on the road 24/7, has time to "do the homework." Most don't even know what the homework is, or where to find it, let alone how to do it. This is why playing this financial game of investing and building wealth will hurt you if you don't understand it. This is a wealth trap because the game is being played against you if you struggle to understand how the financial game works. Remember, financial insiders are being paid to give you advice that benefits the industry, not you. That is the game.

The real name of the game is who is indebted to who, so the more you know or own, the more leverage and power you have in this game of money. This is an insight that is in the industry's best interest not to reveal, because it keeps the financial wheel spinning. To break free of this wealth trap, you must increase your own financial literacy, and think outside of the box. If you want to break free of this wealth trap, you have to become an owner and see opportunities with your mind, not just with the information that is popular and fed to you like breadcrumbs on a trail to nowhere. The solution is to always self-educate first, even if it is to simply learn what to look out for when getting professional help. Remember, nothing is free in this world, and financial advice can often be expensive. If the financial information you receive is considered *popular*, and if you give it all the power to inform you of what you know, then it's probably a *wealth trap.*

Wealth trap #3
"Land a high-paying job or career."

Most people assume that their best odds to becoming wealthy are to land a high-paying job, win the lottery, or invest (X)% of their money monthly in a retirement account. On the contrary, your best odds are building a business and using leverage to purchase cash-producing assets, but most people are afraid to do that because they prefer the stability of receiving a paycheck working for others.

> **There is no certainty in life—only opportunity.**
>
> —Vendetta

Here are the odds of becoming rich, applying the strategies mentioned above:

- *Becoming a business owner*

  Odds: 1,000 to 1

- *Working and investing $800 a month for 30 years*

  Odds: 1,500,000 to 1

Winning the lottery

Odds: 12,000,000 to 1

The truth of the matter is, the odds are stacked against you if you are not actively approaching ways to increase your income and control your money. Simply relying on a standard, safe career to be your economic savior, or sitting around waiting to win that financial lottery, or even retiring your money hoping to someday have financial security—all are a wealth trap in this new monetary world. In the new economy, it is more about how you control your capital than it is about any of these traps disguised as sound financial strategies. The odds to building wealth through these strategies mentioned are immense. Controlling your money and increasing your income streams will be the only control and certainty you will have.

Wealth trap #4
"Take out a student loan"

If you're financially impoverished, and looking for a way up the economic mobility ladder for you and your family, financial pundits will recommend getting an education as a viable solution to achieve increased financial access in America. The media will show you a list of schools that house the best and brightest. Society talks you through the outdated process of obtaining wealth, and you begin to sip the Kool-Aid. Top 10 in this and top 50 in that, your ambition for greatness guides you to the best schools and universities. Only problem; it does the same thing for the other 99% of the population. Supply and demand 101—as more people become interested in seeking out higher education, the cost of higher education goes up (see why I call this advice a form of *financial McDonald's*?). This kind of advice is why the cost of education has increased higher than any other asset class to date. It's become a psychological drug that subconsciously states, "If you want to achieve wealth, you have to pay for it."

> *Question:*

Well, what if I cannot afford the high cost of higher education? What am I supposed to do?

> *The popular financial solution:*

*Take on education debt in order to get a degree that will **probably** allow you to advance economically.*

> *My response:*

Is this considered a form of good debt? I think not. How are you supposed to advance in life with an invisible shackle on your ankle in the form of student loans? Especially if there is no guarantee for employment in your desired field, or if you don't know who you are or what you really want to do after completing school.

**The average person changes careers 11
or more times in their lifetime.**

—Bureau of Labor Statistics

Financial matter, meet financial anti-matter. What happens when these two elements meet? Absolutely nothing! No productivity, only earning to pay it back, subconsciously preparing you for a poor or middle-class outcome in life. The outcome of earning to pay off debt and ignorance to what is considered good debt and what is not.

Wealth trap #5
"FOMO (Fear of Missing Out)"

What is driving the market right now is the antithesis of sound investing; it is the fear of missing out. Basically, fear of being late to the party, of not buying the latest cryptocurrency, IPO, or property before the music ends and you miss out on the deal of a lifetime (*I use the word* deal *here loosely*). Financial media has also played a role in maximizing the impact of the FOMO investment strategy. It is interesting when our mainstream financial media and gurus constantly remind us that a certain large cap index, like the S&P 500, a certain stock, like Amazon, and a specific category, like the NASDAQ, have achieved all-time highs and enticing returns, and we wonder why our more diversified portfolio isn't behaving in a similar fashion. The truth is, it is hard to be content with a diversified strategy when every media outlet constantly reminds us how much we are missing out on the stellar performance that could be obtained if only we had a non-diversified portfolio that invested only in the sector or category that is currently on fire! This cognitive game creates a sense of unease and anxiety and, as a result, forces us to speculate, or turn our money over to the so-called financial experts.

This fanatic investing behavior extends externally and well beyond the paper markets. Someone sees her neighbor making a boatload of cash, which entices her to jump on the money train and invest out of speculation and hype, as opposed to real fundamentals and market analysis. The fear of missing out is an insidious and substantially lethal financial emotion. Although, rarely addressed in behavioral finance, this psychological state of being ruins the overall fundamental health of the economy and the stock market, attributing to boom and bust cycles and increased levels of depression and dissatisfaction. I hope you begin to realize the correlation between popular wealth traps and the FOMO strategy. This strategy is a sure way to set yourself back not only financially, but mentally and emotionally as well. Don't fall for this trap. The solution: equanimity and seeing the opportunity of money with your mind, not with your eyes.

Wealth trap #6
"Look rich"

"I'm not broke, hell no!"

I've noticed that in American culture, there's a stigma (and therefore a deep shame) in either being broke, or being perceived as broke. It's like it's the ultimate failure of the soul and almost irredeemable. "Fake it until you make it" or "Look the part" is common advice given to grow your personal brand, and also to achieve wealth and monetize your influence. I'm sure you've heard these phrases before, whether through the media or from your peers, and you probably accept it as a universal law. I am also pretty sure you know someone who looks rich simply by appearance. You know, the guy who drives around in a new Bentley or Maserati and lives in a luxurious condo with an HOA fee that equals another mortgage. The goal is to wear the wealth on his sleeve for all to see. But are these obviously wealthy people really rich? Very few are. If you analyze the majority of these people, applying this wealth trap, and look at their personal financial statements, an entirely different story is revealed. Some are highly leveraged to the hilt, while others are working to spend their paycheck or income on things to make them seem more financially stable than they really are. The advice to look wealthy creates a wealth trap that is extremely dangerous to one's mental and financial health.

These types of people are one bad economy, or income loss, away from financial ruin and a fatal shot to the ego.

The solution to combat this psychological urge for societal appreciation and acceptance is equanimity and a strong sense of self-worth. It's good to look great for yourself, but the difference between looking good for you, versus looking good to others, is drastic. If you are looking good for you, you can control your impulses, because the response internally lasts a lot longer than the response from society. Society's response is fickle and emotions are ever changing, so appearing to appease the crowd will cause you to constantly adjust, or increase your efforts to match short attention spans. This is a financial disaster, and is likely attributed to a never-ending dependence on money and income.

Wealth trap #7
"Don't take risks, and don't make any mistakes"

"In your pursuit of wealth, don't take any risks, and whatever you do, *do not* make any mistakes." God is the only person who can accomplish such a remarkable feat. As for our ability to accomplish this advice? I am not too sure. If this is the criteria for acquiring wealth in the eyes of our mainstream financial media, then odds are they are setting us up for a life of mediocrity and dependence. This philosophy of perfection is cognitively reinforced from our time in the education system to the workforce. This is why I am not surprised that the same philosophy penetrates the financial industry as well, with statements like, "It's better to turn over your money to an expert so you don't mess up," as if we are children who can't commute to school without a parent. In a way, the tone of this philosophy is that of a person who is protecting us from ourselves. As if we cannot be trusted with the money that we worked extremely hard for. Shielding us from the inevitability of failure and mistakes ultimately creates a larger dependence upon the so-called experts who are part of a small cadre of an exclusive group able to handle the most fragile monetary possession of life—our money.

Now, there is a difference between getting financial advice and falling victim to mainstream financial rhetoric, such as being considered financially illiterate if you opt out of investing your money in a 401k, or being called foolish if you decide to be your own boss instead of working for someone else to determine your paycheck. In order to avoid this subconscious trap, and achieve wealth in our country, you must learn to take risks and understand that mistakes are a necessary part of the game, and of learning and of living in general. The true secret is to learn how to mitigate your risk, taking small but calculated ones, and just not making, but learning from your mistakes. If you can master this, then a successful financial outcome is destined to come your way. Fail small and fast and always be open to learning from your mistakes are the keys to succeeding and achieving your goal to build wealth.

Wealth trap #8
"Owning a house that you live in is BETTER than renting"

Not necessarily. Wait, I know what you're probably thinking. *Jeremiah, you're going mad.* Please, let me argue my case. When you're filling out an application to secure a loan, whether it be for a car or a business loan, the lender will ask on the application what your net worth is, *EXCLUDING* your personal home. Why do you think that is the case? Allow me to explain; it's because the home that you own and occupy is considered to be a LIABILITY.

*Whether you're renting money from the bank via a mortgage, or
renting space from a landlord, you're still renting!*

If you're buying a house, and plan on living in it for 30-plus years, then fine, it makes perfect sense. Go ahead a buy that house to live in. However, if you plan on moving within 15 years, which is what the typical buyer of a single-family home does, then you are only really paying the interest. You don't truly start paying down the mortgage until after about 20 years of ownership. Plus, over the course of those 30 years of paying your mortgage, you will be paying double the purchase price of the home because of interest added to the principal. But I know what you're thinking next. *What about appreciation!?* Yes, it is possible to experience your home's appreciation. However, you will have to time the market perfectly and hope that when that time comes, there isn't a recession or correction that impedes your ability to sell at a profit. Not to mention, due to inflation, and usury (paying off only interest), if you sell, it will be highly unlikely to buy back in the same neighborhood, as many people have experienced throughout history. So, you can see why owning a home to live in can be considered a wealth trap.

QA: What about the tax write-offs that come with homeownership?

A: What about it? Why would you want to get into debt that you're paying for, just to experience a write-off? Unless you own multiple dwellings or have a substantial salary in the millions, the subsidies won't justify the debt incurred.

QA: Is it better to rent?

A: The answer is always "it depends." What I am offering is relief that you don't have to get caught up in a wealth trap of homeownership. Buying, paying for, and maintaining a home that you occupy is a major commitment, and should be handled with care. If you want to buy, then buy smart and make sure other people are paying for it.

Note: There is also an option of buying a multifamily unit, where you are renting one unit and having the income from the other unit subsidize your payment.

Wealth trap #8
Don't touch your 401k!?

Don't touch it! Or should you? This is one of the things that make people cringe. The thought of taking out money from their 401k account before retirement is almost like touching a hot stove! I attribute this to deceptive marketing and intimidating penalty laws that employers and *banksters* use to hold onto your money for longer in order to continue making money on your money. However, once you are fluent in financial product evaluation, meaning that you can look at the things you own, such as your IRA, 401k, and other accounts, you won't be that impressed with your returns on your 401k. Would you believe that, historically, 401k's have only returned less than 4% (*according to* Times)? That's a small percent return for leaving a large chunk of your money in an account that lasts almost 40% of your entire life! So this paradigm, this idea, that you can't access the cash in your 401k without paying huge penalty fees and heavy taxes, is completely false! I will show you how you can still have your 401k, and get access to the cash you need. I am truly surprised that this is something that is NOT disclosed, nor a popular option in mainstream financial advice and information.

Here is a different tactic; borrow from your 401k. When people think of borrowing from their 401k, they think they are either going to pay huge penalty fees or get taxed on the money withdrawn. That is absolutely not the case! You are loaning yourself money. You make a loan to yourself and set your own interest rate on the money you borrow. Yes! Instead of going to the bank or using a credit card with interest rates ranging anywhere from 7% to 22%, you are accessing your money and charging yourself a percentage that you can afford. By borrowing from your 401k, you are essentially becoming your own bank, while paying yourself back with interest. In other words, you keep all of your money, and leverage it at the same time. It's a win-win! But likely something mainstream financial media won't reveal.

Money isn't loyal or neutral

The reason why many of these wealth traps, established through the media and social currency, prevent us from achieving financial free-dom and wealth, is because of a simple principle created alongside the emergence of fiat currency. This is the notion that money is *not* loyal, *nor* is it neutral. There was a time when all you had to do in your quest to keep money was to leave it alone in an interest-bearing savings account, or in your house that you live in. There was also a time when you were guaranteed a consistent paycheck as a result of a city job or sitting in a cubicle for 48% of your entire lifespan. But today, when the world is changing around you, and money is becom-ing digitized debt causing boom and bust cycles in perpetuity, it will be extremely difficult to gain wealth, let alone stay ahead of your money. Tie this in with outdated financial information and rheto-ric that contradicts an ever-changing monetary environment that is our new reality, and you have a population of debtors working for money, only to have their money disappear into the debt loads that they accumulated in the first place from traps disguised as advice to create financial freedom. This is a gerbil-like financial strategy, which keeps us on a spinning wheel of chasing a dollar controlled by the dollar creators. It's quite easy to keep pushing that dollar up as you struggle more and more to catch it on an economic wheel they call opportunity.

Banks bank on themselves, not you

"Banking on you" requires you to first discover why the banks "bank" on themselves. A bank is good for keeping your capital in it to pay your monthly bills and other immediate expenses. However, when it comes to anything else, including your emergency fund, your money should be parked elsewhere! I am going to reveal why.

You want your money to grow, correct? If you're thinking about parking your money in a bank, giving the bank permission to invest and lend out your money, let's see how well that strategy aligns with your goals of growing your wealth. In order to determine how quickly it would grow, you would need to follow a financial formula called the rule of 72. Here's how the rule of 72 works: divide the number 72, by the interest rate you will receive say (e.g., 1% or .01), and the answer will be the number of years it would take for your investment or capital to double in value.

➢ Divide the interest rate by 72 in order to see how long it will take your money to double:

YOU

Interest rate	Years to double	Account
0.01	7200	Your savings account
0.035	2057	CD
0.25	288	standard bank IRA

Now let's compared that to the length it takes banks to make a return:

BANK

Interest rate	Years to double	Loans
4.14%	17	Auto loan
5.50%	13	Mortgage rates
22.99%	3	Credit cards (*bad credit*)

Let me put it to you like this: If you are banking on savings, money market accounts, and CDs, you will never see your money double in your lifetime, nor your children's, nor your children's children's lifetime. Yet, the bank will give you a credit card and see their money double every three years. How is this possible? The reality is, the fractional reserve banking system is in the business of profiting off of your money. They profit by leveraging your savings in order to lend it to someone at interest, who will pay them enough to cover your cash, and give them a profit. Your job is to be your own bank. Read on to find out how.

Get your lazy money a J.O.B.!

The irony is, that with all of the wealth traps, all of the social economic barriers that are out there, there is still a way to climb the economic ladder to wealth. In order to get off the hamster wheel, and start truly making money, you must first acknowledge that you are indeed on a wheel, and shift your mind-set to own the economic wheel. You do this by ditching the savings account mind-set. I am not saying ditch the savings account; I am only pointing to the fact that you must put your savings to work. It's time to ditch the savings account mind-set and get your money a J.O.B. instead!

Your money is lazy, useless, and worthless, just sitting on your couch or under your mattress. It needs to get up and unlock its true potential, which is simply to make more of itself. Should you have a savings account or a reserve set of cash just in case of an emergency? Absolutely. However, just simply saving without allowing your capital to make more money friends for you is not sustainable. Inflation, gas, and innovation increase at rates far faster than savings would. So when you're trying to save every penny until you retire, you are setting yourself up to be that gerbil running in that spinning wheel. Don't be a gerbil. Instead push to be an owner of assets that pay you while you wait for your capital to grow!

Ownership is wealth trap repellant

Wealth traps are like bugs you never see that creep up on you and bite you while you're sleeping. I personally hate bugs. Especially ones disguised as sound financial advice like, "Student loans can be an asset" or "Save," without any other plan to put your money to work for you. The only real wealth trap repellant one must have is ownership. Ownership, whether through an investment property, businesses, intellectual property, stocks, land, or any other hard or soft asset that enables you to monetize it, is a sure way to stay current with or even supersede the growth rate of our economy and money. Through ownership, you have the ability to determine your price if there deems a demand for it. You also have the ability to monetize the asset that you own.

Ownership grants you the ability to do things like:

- Renting out what you own

- Licensing it *(having someone pay to use the name of your asset)*

- Selling it for more than you bought it for

- Using it as collateral in order to borrow capital

- Passing it down to your loved ones

- Building on top of your underlying asset to create more assets

Feel free to think of three other benefits that ownership has:

- _____

- _____

- _____

The control you have with ownership opens you up to an endless amount of financial growth and possibility. Ownership and financial control is what separates the economic haves from the have nots. Without the power of ownership, you are left stuck, limited, and financially enslaved to the rules of money within our monetary system. Consumer-driven debt via high balance credit cards, or any other liabilities, are the shackles. Through developing an ownership mentality, you are able to think like a producer and, as a result, leverage the cash flow from what you own to pay for the things you don't. It's just that simple. It's not rocket science or a complicated math equation. It is more about the psychological and behavioral attributes, than it is about how good you are at math or a degree in finance. Having a high EQ, which enables you to delay instant gratification, is a common trait that all owners display. Owners subconsciously understand how capital works and how spending cash on anything but an asset or necessary expenses is a wasted effort as it relates to economic growth. So the next time you land on that lump sum of cash or consider what to do with that money you saved, keep this in mind. You want to convert most of that cash acquired and invest it in an economic asset.

CHAPTER 3

THE FUTURE OF INVESTING

The greater fool theory

Contrary to what popular financial rhetoric would say, if there is
an asset—whether oil, technology stocks, cryptocurrency, or real
estate—that doesn't produce cash flow for you, then it is NOT . . . I
repeat . . . it is NOT an asset! If you are buying something hoping to
sell it to a bigger fool than you, for more than what you purchased
the asset for, it is called *speculation*. Can you make money speculating? Sure, you can! There are many people who make money at the
casino every day. However, would you recommend gambling at the
casino as a plausible financial strategy? My guess is probably not!

But, for some strange reason, this form of popular financial insight has sort of bulldozed its way into the economic philosophy of our society. In order to avoid being the greater fool, we must re-learn the notion of investing and follow the new rules of investing.

The new 80/20 rule

Forget the old rules related to investing. Following the new 80/20 rule in investing will allow you to not only preserve, grow, and protect your wealth, but will enable you to catch the big fish of investing—profiting off of the speculative unicorns. It's normal to invest in your favorite technology stock, start your own start-up that could potentially be a billion-dollar disruptor, or flip property, hoping to sell for much more than what you bought it for before the economic music ends. However, the success rate of non-fundamental investing is far and few between and requires a ton of expertise and luck. The reality is, you have to be a master at failing fast and small, because the experience gained from these failures will be the education you need for success. The new 80/20 rule of investing means that you are investing 80% of your money in fundamental and cash flowing investments (whether stocks or bonds) and the other 20% on speculative investing. This means that with 80% of your investing money, every purchase of an asset that you make has to instantly start returning cash back to you. Whether through rent roll, dividend payments, or business revenue, you must insure that you are earning cash flow from your investments. The other 20% of the money you are investing can be spent on more speculative investments including unicorn start-ups, emerging markets, that new Airbnb common stock, Amazon stock, or any other new thing that might be considered big. No different from going to the casino. But that is human nature—some have the urge to invest in the next big thing (e.g., cryptocurrency or any other asset class). Do it if you like. Just please make sure that you use my 80/20 rules.

Question:

If you lose 50% of your money, how much do you have to make in gains (%) to break even?

Answer:

If you said 100%, you are correct!

I am pretty sure you're wondering why I presented this question to you. This is because the average loss for an actively managed stock fund was 41% in 2008 (crash of '08), according to Morningstar. Even large-cap mutual funds and small-cap mutual funds experienced a substantial decline at about 38%. This means the average investor would have had to double his money just to break even! Even with all of the gains experienced to date, many people are still struggling to recoup their initial investment. With stocks back at all-time highs, and with macroeconomic issues arising, will we experience a similar drastic loss in the future? In order to avoid a negative outcome similar to 2008, you need to understand the new rules of investing.

The number one rule of money; don't lose it.
The number two rule, don't forget rule #1.

—Warren Buffett

If you haven't noticed, we are in a new monetary world. This is a world of ever increasing inflation, lower for longer interest rates, and of course asset bubbles. The culprit—the Federal Reserve with its lowering and raising interest rates, along with its fiat currency being backed by no real tangible asset outside of a promise to pay it back through taxing incomes. According to many economists, this has been the longest period of interest rate *suppression* in over 5000 years! To put this into perspective, the people working within the central banks were not even born or privy to see the outcome of the last time this happened. My guess is, at this point they're sort of winging it.

> *Interest rates are like gravity to a stock price and as they go down, stocks inevitably go up.*
>
> —Warren Buffett

New rules of stocks and bonds

Here is why it is so important to understand the history of stocks and bonds in order to master the game of investing. Back in the late 1950s and early 1960s, stocks paid higher dividends than bonds in order to entice investors to take a risk to own an equity. If a bond would yield a 5% coupon on its 10-year maturity, then stocks will pay a higher dividend rate, say 7%. This was great if you wanted a higher return, but investing in a stock meant that you had to analyze the payout yourself, as opposed to the bond having a fixed and stable maturity payout.

Owning a government bond has always been deemed a safe investment by financial pundits and purveyors of popular financial advice. This is because owning corporate and government bonds represents their debt and agreement to pay bondholders interest and to return their principal after a certain maturity date (or period). Stockholders were always last in line in the event of a liquidation. This is why bonds are technically considered safer than stocks. But are they?

- *Here's how the rules are changing*: The goal is to buy something that, over time, is going to return cash back to you. So, with interest at an all-time low and bonds returning basically nothing, while companies are producing much higher rates of returns, being told from a financial advisor to do the classic 60/40 allocation (60% stocks, 40% bonds) is financial suicide. It's almost idiotic to own long-term bonds (unless they are corporate bonds) in this low-rate environment. Your financial planners, advisors, and experts aren't wrong, but the antiquated strategy they are promoting in this new monetary environment is.

- *Corporate debt is the new bond*: This option is also a financial gem, hidden from popular financial advice and information. Since a BB (double B) or BBB (triple B) bond is serviced before a corporation pays a dividend on a common stock, you can own up the balance sheet of a corporation, ensuring a guaranteed payment, and protection of your principal in the event of a worst-case scenario of a bankruptcy. If you own a stock that goes to zero, or files for bankruptcy, you will be at risk of losing the entire principal amount plus some on your investment. Owning a corporate bond, preferred stock, convertible and floating rate note will allow you to avoid these perils of owning equities.

Quick tip: Given this new form of fiscal policy, there is a way to understand how to profit on lower as well as higher interest rates as it pertains to investing. In a higher interest rate environment, deflation is in control, which means the following will occur:

1. Decrease in asset prices, or a *correction*

2. Stocks, bonds, and real estate all *on sale*

3. Applicability of the *buy low, sell high* model

In a lower interest rate environment, inflation is in control, which means that the following will occur:

1. Increase in *inflation*

2. Increase in *asset prices* (home values, stock market, etc.)

3. Ability to *leverage debt* to increase your wealth

Simply buying stock is NOT investing:

Volatility, a word commonly used by financial analysts as they describe today's market conditions. This word is prodigious if you're a day or spot trader dipping in and out of positions and anticipating market fluctuations. However, it seems to me as if this word has pierced through the minds of retail and long-term investors as well. To this group of investors, the word is frightening and has them wondering what to do on a daily basis. But why is that? Why is the average retail and long-term investor worried about price fluctuations in the market?

My take is that these investors do not know what they are buying. If you own stocks like you would a house or a business producing a positive net profit, it is highly unlikely that you would get a day-to-day quote or weekly update on the price. The truth is that in any business and investment, the true value of the investment should be how well it is able to deliver cash to its shareholders and owners, not just the price of the security or investment. As long-term investors, our investment philosophy relating to volatility should change if we are looking at it from this perspective. The reality is, markets are always subject to downturns and upswings and anything can happen, especially if there are extraordinary shifts on a macro level.

> *Profits are made when you buy, NOT when you sell.*
>
> —*Rich Dad, Poor Dad*

The idea of people taking an interest in buying real estate, a stock, index, or mutual fund based on the thought of selling it for more is mind-boggling to me. This strategy is not investing; it is flipping, speculation, and most likely the reason why people average 7% annual returns or less over time (4% or less if you add in inflation). If you're investing, my advice is, you should look to the business or underlying asset's ability to produce cash flow to determine whether or not it's a good investment. When you're just looking at the price of something, then you avoid the asset's core function, which is to produce a consistent return of cash to you on the money you invested into it.

Here are some examples:

- Looking at an apartment building to determine how much you could rent it out for to give you a profit or high cash-on-cash return.

- Analyzing farmland to determine whether it grows produce that you could sell at a profit.

- Looking at the business's financial statements, industry trends, and how often it returns cash back to its shareholders.

In my opinion, any investment that can potentially lose 90% of all of its value with a stroke of pen, whether through a policy change or regulation, should not even be called an investment! The problem is, many people get charmed by lots of price action and hype and confuse the momentum and liquidity of these speculative gains with it being a great investment. I personally don't care if it's the next Facebook, Uber, or even Bitcoin, if it is not returning cash to me, it is a speculation. This is not to say that I won't take part in any new tulip mania that is introduced. I mean, the gains during that time were exponential and massive. However, I will only play with money I can STAND to lose! I'm not leveraging my hard-earned money, mortgaging my house, or borrowing on a margin in order to play a game of financial musical chairs, and neither should you. Instead, I've applied simple rules of investing and protecting my profits from what seems like the inevitable events of volatility, pullbacks, and economic downturns. Allow me to share them with you.

Here are the seven most important and *basic rules of investing*:

1. **"F" the story**: Never more than 20% of your money should be in any one asset class, no matter how great the hype is! I don't care if it's the next new cryptocurrency, a friend's business, new technology stock, bonds, gold, silver, property, or any other thing that you deem an asset. Good asset column and sectoral diversification, including CASH on hand, is crucial to your economic survival.

2. **Patience is a virtue**: Never buy or sell ALL at once. Instead you should place incremental orders when you purchase stock, and buy real estate in stages. This allows you to time your moves in the market better and avoid drastic shifts in the price as you begin to make your moves. Discipline trumps conviction.

3. **Be greedy when others aren't**: Have you ever heard the saying, "Bulls make money, bears make money, pigs get slaughtered"? Well, there is a reason why this rule stands the test of time in regards to investing. However, here is where I digress. I think you should be prudent when others are greedy, but greedy when others aren't. This allows you to take advantage of boom and bust cycles in any market and be on the positive end of any investment cycle.

4. **Know the difference between an opportunity and a bad deal**: It is important to know and understand the difference between an investment that just slid in price due to macro-level events, and a damaged investment altogether. Whether you are buying a traditional brick-and-mortar business, investing in real estate, or buying stocks, understanding this simple philosophy will prevent you from

enduring monster financial losses. For example: If you noticed that J.C. Penney stock, a company that once dominated the retail space, is down in price, find out why. If its financials indicate that the company may be going insolvent, listen to them. If you see new technology replacing this industry, listen to that.

5. ***Diversify across different asset classes:*** Investing in one asset class and feeling that you are diversified will subject you to financial losses in the event of an economic downturn in that cycle. Instead, focus on the power of your asset column, for instance, businesses, real estate, paper assets, and cash! That's right, I even deem cash an asset simply because it's capital, and the true nature and value of capital is that it makes more of itself. Try not to invest in only one market, but spread your risk across asset columns. This way, you can protect your wealth in the event of an economic downturn. In fact, take the winnings of your highest producing asset class, and use the appreciation from it to buy more undervalued assets—assets that have been affected by a macroeconomic downturn. This is how you build wealth, even on a shoestring budget. Diversifying your asset class, not just sector diversification of stocks.

Diversification is the only free lunch in investing.

—Kevin O'Leary

6. ***Pay the TAX:*** Don't be afraid to pay the tax man on profits you've earned. It's better to take a profit when you're up then ride the losses. The rules of buy, hold, and pray, no

longer apply, so if the opportunity presents itself and you have realized gains, don't be afraid to take some off of the top and play with the house money. Remember, a profit on paper is not the same as profit in your bank account. This is how you will be able to beat the market.

7. *Panic is not a strategy:* I remember the 2010 flash crash when the stock market went down close to 1,000 points within a day. My mother called me asking if she should liquidate her shares and I immediately told her not to. It was unwise for anyone to liquidate out of panic when macro events like that happen. My advice is, the next time the market takes a hit, and I can confidently say it will, don't panic. It is a proven fact that the most money is made when investors buy during market dips and even economic downturns. Panic is the antithesis of discipline. Sell-offs and depressed investment prices can in fact produce massive and even infinite returns, but always remember to look into the investment in order to determine whether it is worth pursuing.

Although I have provided some of my best principles of investing in order to avoid and withstand volatility and price fluctuations in any market, if you are not emotionally and psychologically fit for investing, you should refrain from investing altogether, or simply hand over your money to a professional (I know we've all seen the outcome to this strategy). Either way, a common emotion that is needed to survive in the world of investing is equanimity. You have to have the mental composure as well as the emotional intelligence to confidently make a decision and stick to it. Fundamentally, you should always know what you're buying. I believe more people would be financially confident and decisive—and have equanimity—if they would simply be fully educated on what they are really buying (which is pieces of businesses), as opposed to turning their money over or using the buy, hold, and pray strategy. Cultivating this emotion and your financial literacy will allow you to not only earn money by investing, but generate infinite returns!

Only Listen to a Company's Financial Statements.

In my view, the only way to get capital appreciation is to find companies that are growing. My criteria for growth has little to do with a company's earnings report, especially in a low interest rate environment. In this environment, companies can easily artificially inflate their earnings with this report by leveraging borrowed cash (debt) and buying other companies with it. They don't have to reinvest the money back into the company on property, plant, employees, or equipment for real intrinsic growth. These companies can simply acquire other companies, lay off workers, and show that their earnings have increased, even with antiquated technology or business models. It is the equivalent to an athlete using steroids, as opposed to working out naturally in order to get gains.

Instead, I find companies that have free cash flow! In other words, the company has to display free cash flowing in after capital expenditures. If you always look at the free cash flow of any investment, it will keep you safe and confident. Find simple deals in which you can understand the business model and see an easy path to revenue—that is the key to financial abundance in investing.

DON'T *buy the story, buy the cash!*

One thing that I enjoy about this strategy is that you can see through the story of any company or investment. There is no vision, there is no pitch on how this new company will revolutionize the world but your money is needed in order to do it . . . there is just CASH FLOW. This is the only thing I listen to when it comes to making an investment in any asset class outside of *physical* gold and silver (which are insurance policies on fiat currency). The money coming in is the only story you should see and hear. This is the holy grail of investing.

Side note: Whenever you're investing, you should have a tiny element of fear. You should make the assumption that whatever you're investing in, whether it be stocks, bonds, businesses, commodities (especially commodities), there is some probability that you will lose it. It could become zero, which is why you always need to have a reserve, some cash set aside so that if everything fails, you are still okay.

Here is how I'd choose to find and analyze a great company. I simply follow and analyze the company's P&L statement, which exposes whether or not the company is profitable, the balance sheet to determine the company's net equity, and the cash flow statement to check the life blood of the company, which is the cash flowing in or out of it.

Your analysis should look like this:

- *Income statement*: Summary on how any company incurs (or gets) its revenue and expenses.

  ➢ Goal: Net *income* should always be **POSITIVE**

- **Balance sheet**: *Shows a company's assets vs. its liabilities and the difference is called net equity.*

  ➤ <u>Goal</u>: Net *equity* should always be **POSITIVE**

- **Cash flow statement**:

  ○ *Operating net cash flow*: **POSITIVE**

    ✳ *How much money the company is generating every year. Obviously, the goal is to see a positive number here.*

  ○ *Investment activities*: **NEGATIVE**

    ✳ *This number represents the company investing back into the company. Negative means the company is reinvesting capital gains back into itself.*

  ○ *Financing activities*: **NEGATIVE**

    ✳ *You want the company to either buy back its shares, increasing the stock price, or distribute dividends to the shareholders.*

Here are other metrics to consider:

- **Price to earnings**: *Determines if the stock or company is overvalued.*

  ○ *No more than 15 – 18 times the company's annual earnings*

- **Price to book**: *Determines the real value or book value of the stock or company.*

  ○ *No more than 2 times book value is the ideal number*

- **Debt to equity ratio**: *Measures the riskiness of a company by comparing its debt to the amount of equity it has.*

  ○ *Ratios at .04 or lower are considered ideal metrics*

Note: Using a stock screener (e.g., *Google stock screener*) will allow you to input these numbers in weeding out the speculative stocks from the ones really producing profits and returning free cash.

The key to life is the check coming in. It's the only thing that I look for in any investment strategy, and so should you. If a company fails to meet the above criteria, it will be extremely challenging for me to invest in it. The money would have to be money that I would normally gamble with at the casino, and the investment would be a whimsical one. The cash flow from any investment will be the only thing that has the potential to be a certainty in your life. It will be the only friend, equality, security, or cute pet you're going to have when you're old and wrinkled. Listening to popular financial advice from CNBC and the like will manipulate us to invest in the next IPO, crypto, or biotech company that we know nothing about. This is not investing. This is called buying the hype. I am only helping you to spot the difference.

HINT: How to analyze a quality business?

➢ *Solid earnings growth*

> *Undervalued*

> *Cash rich*

> *Low debt*

> *Growing sales*

Only follow the 1% rule in real estate investing

What if I told you that there is a tool you can use in a moment's notice to quickly analyze any investment property deal? In order to buy cash flowing properties correctly in real estate, it is imperative that you follow this one rule that all successful real estate investors follow, and that is the 1% rule of real estate investing. Following this rule is a great way for you to do a quick analysis on any property that you decide to purchase as an investment.

Let's analyze a real estate deal together, shall we?

Property: $150,000

Cash flow: $1000 per month

Is this a good investment? Yes, or no?

If you said or circled no, then you are beginning to understand the 1% rule in investing in real estate. A 150,000 house that is only going to cash-flow $1000 violates the 1% rule. I'd rather buy two properties instead, that equates to the 150k property that produce $1000 dollars each. This is simply because the two properties at 75k each producing $1000 passes the 1% rule and would double the amount of cash flow received from the 150k house! Again, this enables you to get an initial assessment of an investment property, and is a tool in your arsenal that will help you invest in and buy rental properties. These are things we don't learn in school, not even in real estate school, but is what the wealthy learn through experience.

Produce an Infinite Return

If you ask your financial advisor or banker what a good return on your money should be, odds are they will show you an antiquated, traditionally accepted chart showing you historic and theoretical data of returns ranging from 7% to 10%. These numbers represent industry expectations and returns that a retail investor should have after investing money into the stock market or real estate.

To put this in layman's terms, and using simple numbers:

You put up $1000

You will get a 10% return ($100 return on your money)

In this model, you would need to have your capital invested into the asset in order for the asset to produce money for you. With this strategy, it would take a longer period of time in order to not only recoup your initial investment, but to profit from it entirely. You are not using the power of leverage effectively.

What if I told you that, once again, the information you've been given regarding money is not entirely true. Fortunately for many of us, seeking a 10% yield is considered to be "short change" compared to the strategy I am about to reveal. With a higher financial IQ, we have the ability to not only make money out of nothing, but to also produce income in perpetuity. This process is called producing an *infinite return*. The definition of an infinite return is simple: owning a cash flow producing asset with no money invested into the underlying asset. This is an advanced technique that holds benefits far beyond just a return on your ideas or creative financing. Whether you are interested in owning a single family home or commercial property, the same rules to creating an infinite return apply:

* *Buy the asset using little to none of your own money*

* *Take out your initial investment either through a refinance, HELOC, or hard money loan*

* *Allow the cash flow from the property to pay off the debt and produce a profit for you*

Here is an illustration of the infinite return production strategy (I will use simple numbers to make it easy to understand):

You invest $1000

Initial cash-on-cash return: **limited**

Use power of leverage to get your $1000 back

New cash-on-cash return: **Infinite**

(Because your principal is no longer being invested)

Caution: Real estate is a very finance and management intensive proposition. You have to know your numbers in order to achieve an infinite return in this space. The good news is, it does not require complex math or formulaic equations. You only need simple addition, subtraction, and attention to detail in order to excel with this strategy. Let me simplify it for you: Don't let you eye off the profit. Producing an *infinite return* simply means that you are taking back the cost to own the property and getting cash flow as well. It is a both-and scenario.

Other types of investments that are able to help you produce an infinite return:

- *Your ideas* – Accessing the power of your mind, intellectual property, or creativity to produce something that can yield an infinite return

- *Other people's money or time* (OPM/T) – Raising capital to produce an asset or build a business

- *IPO, ICO, Crowdfunding* – Leveraging the power of your inner network/community in order to get the necessary resources to get your business to scale.

- *Technology* – Creating a value-added product or service and scaling it

- *Options trading* – Allowing you to have the right, but not the obligation, to own a stock at a particular price. This strategy increases your upside (profit) and covers your downside (risk).

- ***Sharing knowledge*** – Either through creating a YouTube channel, training, writing literature, or speaking at events, these are ways to produce an infinite return on your time or money.

The ultimate goal to producing an infinite return would be to either leverage a skill or your idea that would require little or no money to start, or invest your money (following the new rules of investing mentioned) into a cash flowing asset and recouping your money from your investments allowing the still-owned investment to continue to make money for you.

What are some skills or ideas that you could leverage to help you produce an infinite return on your time or money?

Think of 5 and write them down here:

1. _____

2. _____

3. _____

4. _____

5. _____

Have five skills or ideas in mind? Great! You have just created up to five different sources of *income* tailored to you. By completing this simple exercise, you understand the process of developing multiple streams of income.

My goal is to only show you that contrary to what the world shows you, you have something unique to bring to the table and you, too, have the ability to monetize your personal value proposition. Always remember, true value tends to derive from a personal pain point or problem. The problems or obstacles you see in the world can, in fact, provide opportunities that only you have subconscious access to. So trust yourself and don't be afraid to act on the changes or solutions that you want to see in the world. It could be quite profitable.

CHAPTER 4

BLOCKCHAIN: THE NEW FREE MARKET?

I'm sure we've all heard about the catastrophic move that is headed towards the crypto space. This move is contrary to the very essence of this technology's value proposition and could very well disrupt the fabric of this space. I'm talking about the R word—REGULATION! But before we get into why Congress is shaking in their pants by this new wave of freedom that they are unable to control, let's go back and explain both the genesis behind this revolutionary digital money and its innovative technology.

World Money

Since the inception of the Federal Reserve, established in 1913, the world's monetary system has been historically designed to benefit only a few at the expense of the many. As stated in my previous book *Financial Freedom: My Only Hope*, through the creation of *fiat* currency (USD), and rate manipulation from lowering and raising rates from a flick of a switch and policy implementation, the fed transfers wealth from the ordinary person to the people who control and run this monetary game. These masters of the fiat currency game consist of the following:

- Central banks

- Commercial banks

- The financial sector (Wall Street)

- Government & corporations (by borrowing cheap money)

Subtle transition to digital money

The rise of electronic money started with the emergence of wire connections (*wire transfers*), then came a derivative of money known as credit money. Credit money (*credit cards*) was one of the original forms of digital money. The first inception of digital money was in 1950. Diner's Club issued the first credit card, which, interestingly enough, was designed primarily for rich businessmen as a special perk. However, as soon as banks realized there were billions of dollars to be made by issuing credit to the masses, credit cards exploded on the scene, becoming mainstream in less than 10 years! Today, with the help of Visa and bank-issued credit cards, there are over 200 million credit cards in use in the United States alone. Following wires, and credit cards, came direct deposits. The Social Security Administration first offered automatic electronic deposit of money into bank accounts in the early 1970s. Corporations, and other employers, soon adopted this model. Once people became comfortable with the concept of digital money being easier to access than paper money, the practice widely spread. Society started to earn and spend money without even touching it. People began paying bills, transferring money, and sending money electronically, and adopted new innovative technologies such as PayPal and Venmo to send money to and from each other. Centralized digital platforms have been at the forefront today; however, in 2008, something substantially changed.

Introduction of Blockchain Technology

Fast-forward to today and we are staring in the eye of a digital revolution—Blockchain technology. Through the emergence of a revolutionary technology in 2008 called bitcoin, and other alt coins, decentralized digital money will infiltrate society in the future and become the new form of money and free market capital. The transition from a tangible paper currency, to a more abstract one, has in fact been an insidious and covert one. This open-sourced distributed ledger technology is the underlying device that has the power to record every transaction you've made such as:

- The last place you've visited

- Who you last communicated with

- The emails that you've written (poor Hillary)

- All of your financial and personal files

- Even what web pages you've visited in the past (I hope you haven't visited what I think)

With every cryptocurrency incorporating Blockchain technology, you can see why there are so many cryptocurrencies out there. The crypto space is bringing back the free market concept of the best service, price, and most value-added wins. This age-old concept of free market has been kept in circulation by mainstream financial gurus and media. However, you cannot have free market without the fairness of money. Having a central banking system creates a middleman, forcing money to be manipulated through the process of printing currency with no intrinsic value, and of lowering and raising interest on money. However, through the use of Blockchain technology and encryption as a primary source of this new age monetary system, we could remedy this centralized middleman dilemma that is currently plaguing our current economy.

Sorting the good from the bad cryptocurrencies

Cryptocurrency was created to invert the power structure from the centralized entities back into the hands of the individual. We could actually be on the verge of a paradigm shift in currency and trade, which could ignite a new world monetary system. However, with all of the many different cryptocurrencies out there, how do we weed out the good ones from the outright scams and rotten ones? Well! After assessing the cryptocurrency landscape, I've come up with two major mandates for investing in the right cryptocurrency!

1. *Merchant or market adoption:* A cryptocurrency should have some sort of merchant adoption or market penetration. Although merchant adoption is similar to miner adoption, it is simply a matter of understanding the

different outlooks. "Different participant, same rules. The difference is that miners have a speculative sentiment and merchants are conservative." The market and merchants all have three principal aims when it comes to adopting a payment system:

➤ to make money

➤ to save money

➤ to increase awareness

If you can bring them customers and increase their sales while reducing their payment fees, or making life easier altogether, then the rest is a matter of persistence and making it as easy as possible to get them started.

2. ***Protocol/Utility:*** In late 2017, I was invited to attend a cryptocurrency event by my good friend Justin Wu, who is a growth hacker and cryptocurrency expert insider. At the event, there were a ton of other industry experts and I saw it as an opportunity to learn about everything relating to cryptocurrency and the Blockchain space. But there was one guy there who gave me the most compelling yet subtle advice about how to assess any new cryptocurrency. He said that the first question you must always ask is a simple one, "What is the utility?" He added, "I only buy infrastructure!" The utility should always be a value-added component within the underlying cryptocurrency. A good utility offers an infrastructure that can be leveraged to build on top of. Ethereum, for example, allows the use of smart

contracts for decentralized applications (code that can execute transactions without a third party or intermediary) on top of its platform. Eos, the Chinese Ethereum, and Cardano are other infrastructure-based cryptocurrencies. This is a great utility that can prove the currency's viability. No wonder it's one of the top cryptos on the market. You should always know this term if you're looking to own a cryptocurrency.

3. ***Network effect***: Oddly enough, every big multinational company and product started niche and hyper local. As more people within the niche adopted the model, the bigger and more popular the company or product becomes. The same should work in the Blockchain space. There should be somewhat of a network effect and user adoption for the currency to be sustainable. Certain neighborhoods, cities, events, venues, and groups of people that are built around a community of like-minded consumers allowing them to trade freely, quickly, and securely for goods and services that are important in their lives instead of having to rely on the central banks and larger markets to tell them what arbitrary item, be it a copper coin or a plastic dollar, holds value.

Bit of caution: This powerful and innovative technology could either free us or enslave us. I am more than certain that in the future, governments and central banks will want to use this technology to their advantage. Turning over your control in this space, by participating in any government or banking system backed cryptocurrency or distributed ledger, is detrimental and contrary to the very essence of the creation of this technology. If the government or banking system develops a distributed ledger or even a Fed-backed crypto, they will have a power far greater than any fiat currency controlled printing press. They will have the ability to shut you off, regulate what you can and can't buy, control information, control your life, and even freeze you out of the financial system altogether.

The ripple effect

The problem today with the cryptocurrency space is that Wall Street and the financial sector are trying to figure out how they can get a slice of the profits. However, outside of creating bitcoin futures and taxing, it is almost impossible for Wall Street to infiltrate this space because of the way these digital currencies are engineered. The only form of regulation that could exist is the points where you can convert digital money (cryptocurrencies) into nation fiat currencies.

> *Bitcoin can't be regulated.*
>
> —Mike Maloney

We have an opportunity now to have a new world monetary system and use an entirely new and sufficient form of money. However, we are treating this revolutionary technology like we're at the casino. Playing roulette, picking up cryptocurrencies because of its nice-looking logo or promise, and flipping these digital currencies hoping that we don't end up with a 20% or more pullback is not the point of this innovation. If we start using cryptocurrencies as a medium of exchange to buy and sell goods and services, instead of using it simply for speculating and trading amongst other digital currencies, then this will lead us to true freedom and create an authentic and level-free enterprise. Market penetration will be the indicator to look out for as this space continues to grow. There will need to be real utilities and real-world usage for these currencies, if they are to survive and thrive in the cryptocurrency markets. Just speculating will only produce temporary results, and timing your exit could be difficult.

Crypto Tax

It's humorous how we talk about everything but taxes when it comes to the cryptocurrency space. So what I am going to do for you is decode this elusive game of cryptocurrency taxes. Tax season is always the most daunting time of the year, but in the crypto space, it may be straight hell, especially if you are on the opposite end of the gains! If you are preparing for your return, please know this: the IRS labels cryptocurrency as "property," not as "currency." Simply put, you're subjected to the same tax assessment as if you own stocks.

Here is how to file on your holdings.

- Record your transactional history (whenever you bought and sold your positions). This will determine if you have a capital gain.

- Fill out an 8949 form and schedule D.

- Taxed up to 39% (of course, depending on your income).

Remember to always consult with a professional tax attorney or accountant in this area. I am simply offering ubiquitous instructions and public information on how to file in this space.

Crypto Tax Strategies:

Although the cryptocurrency space is so new and hard to understand the various technological nuances incorporated within the blockchain, we know two certainties related to this asset class.

These certainties are as follows:

1. *It is extremely volatile.*

2. *There will be taxes to pay on any gains that you accrue.*

Here is a simple strategy that you can use to ensure you are out of potential trouble with the IRS pertaining to trading cryptocurrency. As you are trading, take 30% of your profits whenever you decide to sell, and set it aside for the IRS. This will relinquish any economic confusion on your end and allow you to track your profit.

These are a few things to consider relating to crypto and taxes:

- Many of us think that if we traded dollars for bitcoin, that we are exempt from paying taxes. However, the IRS is smarter than that, so they deemed crypto-to-crypto trades to be considered a taxable event. Let me elaborate. Let's say I traded bitcoin for Lite coin, Ripple, Eos, or any other cryptocurrency. This is considered a sale (based on IRS guidelines), and could be costly if I'm a frequent trader in this space.

- According to the Commodity Futures Trading Commission (CFTC), cryptocurrency is now classed as a commodity in the U.S. along with gold and oil, which means it will be subjected to the same tax obligations, as if you were trading stocks. Long-term currencies held for a year or more will be taxed less than day trading currencies. The same rules that normally apply to stock trading apply here. This is extremely important information if you are looking to trade in this space.

These are some of the many tax strategies, if you want to remain out of the hair of the IRS. In my opinion, this is the only way that they could regulate and control this digital money. This is a way for the government to insidiously siphon money out of this space and get a piece of the action. The ultimate middlemen, in my opinion.

Tulip mania 2.0?

Is the emergence of this revolutionary technology reforming capitalism? Or, are we reliving tulip mania? You know, when the price of tulips in the Dutch economy, in the 1600s, rose to prices completely insane and unattainable? My guess is, we will soon find out.

The truth is, Blockchain is a revolutionary trust layer that could soon turn the internet and possibly our entire economy into a true free market. Bitcoin, being the first and one of the many underlying platforms with distributed ledger technology, will continue to provide more applications to be built on top of it. Ultimately, whether bitcoin is here 100 years from now or gone tomorrow, its influence and contribution to the overall Blockchain landscape, will only enhance the overall functionality of this space and spearhead new ecosystems to come. Similar to any new phenomenon that eventually sticks, the survival of this industry is heavily dependent upon a collaborative support and confidence from the masses. The 99%, not the 1%. Yes! The future of cryptocurrency and its survival is dependent not on Warren Buffett's opinion, the banks' adoption of it, nor the financial media or government, but through us! The free market, and the people participating in it will determine the next form of money in the future. So, it is your job to ensure, if you want decentralized digital money, to participate and create a network effect around it.

CHAPTER 5

PROTECT YOUR CASTLE: CORPORATIONS

I love traveling. My ultimate goal is to explore every corner on earth and see the many wonders this world has to offer. One unique observation that I discovered through traveling is that this beautiful planet houses a diverse group of people from all walks of life. Although there are so many beautiful people with unique backgrounds, ethnicities, and religions, one thing is for certain—the rich will always have castles shielding themselves from the poor. Now, I know you probably think I am referring to that time you traveled through the poorest part of the island or country in order to get to the main, rich part of it. No, the castle I am referring to is a legal one. It's called a corporation.

*You don't build castles with rock and stone anymore. Today,
you build them with corporations and attorneys!*

—Robert Kiyosaki

Throughout history, the rich had to have physical castles in order to protect themselves from people attempting to steal from them. Today, these castles are in the form of paper and documents called corporations. The harsh reality is that people are people, so if you are trying to become wealthy, there will always be someone who will attempt to steal from you, lie, and cheat. So instead of me handing you a few bricks to build a castle, I will make your life easy and teach you how to use paper and documents to build it instead.

My house is in my name

Ah! The sweet pride of ownership. The sweet joy of having everything in your name from the home that you live in, to the car that you drive, and even all of your money in one checking account. Life is great, isn't it? That is until someone tries to sue you for the smallest occurrence, such as bumping into them with your car, or slipping and injuring themselves in front of the property that is in your name. Being sued for looking at a person the wrong way or even putting your hands on them (I do not condone violence in any way) can also signal a suit. You can even be wiped out by a divorce settlement if your assets are not properly protected. I'm sure you can see why having everything in your name can in fact be detrimental to your overall wealth strategy.

I personally don't want anything in my name! I'd hate to be the one amassing wealth through hard work, blood, sweat, and tears, only to have someone try to take my wealth from me simply because they want what I have. I would rather protect myself by building a castle, or, in this era, setting up a corporation such as the following:

> LLCs

> S corporations

> C corporations

> LPs (Limited partnerships)

The cost of protecting your assets and building your paper *castle* is relatively cheap; less than $1000 max to properly set up and get incorporated and a few hundred dollars a year in order to maintain it. It is a sunk cost; something that needs to be done initially, so that you can avoid incurring a major cost down the road such as a lawsuit or pointless taxation as you begin to accumulate wealth. Creating a corporation allows you to avoid the two biggest monetary predators in the world, which are:

1. *__The government__* - taxes

2. *__People__* - lawsuits from people who want to sue you for their mistakes

If you want to pay less in taxes and have more asset protection, change your mentality from wanting everything in your name to protecting your castle by putting your assets under your corporation.

Corporations are simply insurance on assets

Think of a corporation simply as a form of insurance for your assets. You wouldn't drive your car without insurance, nor would you own a house without it, so why wouldn't you protect the most important thing in your personal profile, your wealth? Setting up a corporation may cost the initial amount plus a couple of bucks each year in order to preserve it, but it is a sunk cost you must bear in order to protect an even larger cost in the future. From lawsuits to garnishment via spousal privileges, these are expenses that could not only cost you, but completely wipe you out! This is way it's imperative that you protect your assets, the machines that fund your livelihood, so that in the end the individual is stuck holding the lawyer fee bag and nothing else.

Corporation, LLC, sole proprietor . . . what is the difference?

The difference has less to do with the different entities themselves, and more to do with taxes and fees associated with incorporating them. However, let's get a more thorough understanding of why someone starting a company might want to choose one corporate structure over another.

Sole proprietor:

Being a sole proprietor is one of the easiest and most cost effective structures to establish. This structure is more for that one or two business owners, who want to set up shop quickly and cost efficiently, allowing them to be business owners without much in the way of fees and regulations. The downside of setting up this way is the minimal liability you will have if the business fails, or if you are subjected to a lawsuit. There is nothing wrong with getting started as a sole proprietor, but if you're looking to protect your castle, then this structure may not be designed for you.

Limited Liability Companies:

This option is what more than 80% of people use when they decide to get into business or start a company. This choice allows a separation between you and your business, bringing on an entity of its own for your business. In other words, any debts incurred by an LLC belong to the LLC itself, rather than to the owners of the company. With regards to taxes, the IRS classifies an LLC as pass-through entities, which means they are only taxed once, at the individual level. The LLC itself pays no taxes. You will need to claim your business profits (or losses) on your individual income tax return, which means an LLC requires less record-keeping than an S-corp! If you decide to go this route, please understand that you will be subjected to pay taxes on the income gained or lost in your LLC.

C & S Corporations:

An S-corp is similar to an LLC in specific situations, particularly when it comes to taxation. S-corporation owners' salaries are often self-determined and taxed as income. The main difference is that dividends can be paid out to the owners, and thus taxed—separately. This can save 10% to 15% in taxes over the course of the year, though bookkeeping and related costs will be higher than they are for an LLC. In all, S-corporations are useful for business owners who wish to pay themselves salaries and who want to take advantage of the tax savings that come with the dividend structure.

My favorite corporate structure.

C-corps are the most common structures used in technology companies and multinational business conglomerates. By establishing a C-corp, you are able to issue stock to multiple investors and get taxed twice. Unlike LLCs or S-corps, the profits or losses aren't passed through to the individual. They are simply taxed at the corporate level. The owners of the operation are subjected to double taxation, which means the company has to pay one tax and the individual has to pay any taxes on his salary plus dividends, if the individual was paid by his corporation. The reason why I love the C-corp structure so much is because there is an easy way to get around this double taxation. Simply do what Mark Zuckerberg (Facebook), Larry Ellison (Oracle), and Jeff Bezos (Amazon) did with their companies; pay yourself $1 and write off as many expenses as you can under your corporation. It creates a win-win, because you can write off items that you use every day like a luxury sports car, a high-end watch or suit, homes, and anything else, under your C-corp, reducing its overall tax liability. All the while, you pay little to no taxes because you paid yourself a small amount ($1) on your personal tax report. This is why I personally love a C-corp formation when building your company or business.

Asset protection in middle America?

There is now a reason to head to the state of Wyoming, other than going for a Kanye West album release party; its healthy and generous corporate tax structure! No wonder Kanye West was in middle America and wanted to fly everyone, first class at that, out to Wyoming just to hear him release songs on his new album. Forget the speculation, I have done the research and will reveal why Wyoming might be the new Delaware. Businesses love Wyoming simply because Wyoming does not have a state or personal income tax, among other benefits. Don't take it from me, let's look at the facts. The state of Wyoming has:

- *NO Personal income tax*

- *Less red tape bureaucracy & restrictions*

- *NO Corporate income tax*

- *NO Inventory tax*

- *NO Gross receipts tax*

- *NO Franchise tax*

- *NO Business or per-capita tax*

- *Sales, property, and inheritance taxes are among the lowest in America*

Out of all of these benefits to get incorporated in the state of Wyoming, the one that attracts me is not even on this list, and that is the *right to privacy.* Since Wyoming has no requirement whatsoever for the names of shareholders to be filed with the state, the filing process allows the owners of the LLC to withhold their names. This is great because the more information about you that appears in the public record, the easier it is for you to become a target of a lawsuit. Incorporating in Wyoming will prevent any disclosures of shareholders, protecting the owner from predatory lawsuits or even the government for that matter.

As you can see, there are numerous Wyoming corporation advantages that make it a better state to do business in. Always remember, no matter if you are moving a company, forming a new one, or looking to purchase, check with your attorney to see if it is the right situation for you and your business entity.

Paradise Island - Offshore it!

What if I told you that there are *new tax havens* outside of the traditional states like Delaware, Nevada, and Wyoming, which some of the most popular American corporations use in order to hide over $60 billion a year. This type of cryptic information is hidden from the popular financial experts and media from by mega-corporations as well as small mom-and-pop companies looking to save on taxes as well. Do you believe this corporate phenomenon is happening? Well, one major way they avoid paying the tax man is by parking their profits overseas. With a 35% tax rate and a tax code encouraging offshoring, who would blame these corporations from hiding money in the Cayman Islands and Bermuda, Switzerland, or Ireland, where there are no taxes at all. Thanks to effective lobbying and savvy lawyers, you have the ability, within the parameters of your company, to exploit the provisions within the tax law. In fact, every other government applauds lowering their corporate tax base to rates that are attractive to many US companies, and that is why these US corporations go there. But why can't your business go there? It's because the information is hidden from you. My job is to unveil this esoteric information. Today, a company can simply move its assets, IP, and other forms of profit transfers, on paper. These maneuvers allow a company to escape the 35% tax base and increase revenue and net profits. No wonder Apple Corporation has close to $400 million trapped overseas tax-free. Your job is to do as Apple does if you want to profit at the same rate as Apple has.

Whether you are offshoring, creating corporations, or setting up strategies like the ones mentioned above, what you are essentially doing is finding loopholes to preserve your money and assets. Unfortunately, due to people taking advantage of these secretive protections, the term *loophole* has had a negative connotation within our society. However, it really comes from the idea of how you protect yourself. The word *loophole* was derived from the holes in castles during the Medieval time period, when people would sneak through and shoot arrows at their enemies through the holes in their castle. Today, the loopholes are set up so you can protect yourself from anyone trying to attack your wealth or the fruits of your labor. Because Vikings in the form of taxes, lawsuits, and bad debt, could at any time attempt to attack your investments. The beginning and end goal of your efforts in building wealth and increasing your passive income should be to protect your assets like the rich.

CHAPTER 6
THE **CREDIT** HACK

There is a study (via Experian) showing that personal credit scores are approaching all-time highs, while overall personal debt—including mortgages, student loans, and auto loans—has also hit a record $12.9 trillion, its largest amount in history! This had me wondering, what if this milestone means people are adopting similar dangerous habits that led to all of the credit bubbles in the past? With FICO scores at all-time highs, does that mean we have learned from these past mistakes? Only time will tell. In the meantime, let's continue to learn how credit works and how we can get our FICO scores to scrape the 800 mark.

Navigating the Game of Credit

Based on what you've just read, I know you're probably wondering what is credit, really, and why is it such a big deal if it is heavily related to the increase in overall consumer debt loads? Simply put, credit scores act as your adult report card. Yes, even as adults, we are still evaluated like children. Popular consensus and mainstream financial experts will point to credit reports as a measurement of how financially responsible and competent we are. But that is simply not the case. You can have an 800+ credit score and still be in massive student loan or overall debt. A credit score is designed to only reveal how well you manage debt. Nothing more, nothing less.

Lenders, before lending you money, need to know two important things about you:

1. Whether you *can* pay back the loan.

2. If you *will pay it back on time.*

Theoretically, credit scores and FICO scores (or **F**air **I**saac and **Co**mpany scores) will reveal this type of information to lending institutions. Based on my experience, however, it seems as if these reports are secret indicators of our economic status and financial resilience, or lack thereof.

> *Credit is bad only if you don't know how to use it.*
>
> —Jeremiah Brown

Ironically, good credit is a huge factor of your ability to become or remain financially successful. This is because the better your credit score is, the more leverage you are able to use, the less interest you pay on borrowed money, and the easier it is to receive the best rates, terms, and payment options on money. This could be the difference between getting access to capital to enhance your economic mobility, and being an economic slave. Understand that credit is simply a game that, unfortunately, could cost you if you don't play it right (pun intended). However, I'd rather take an elevator to wealth than walk up flights of stairs any day. Having good credit, by design, allows you to gain access to that financial elevator, creating an easier way to reach wealth, but only if you use its privileges the right way.

Credit scores, however, only access the information contained in your credit reports. They never consider your income or your personal characteristics. This would be known as profiling and is absolutely illegal. Instead, each agency uses the following to calculate a score:

- *Credit History* – To put into laymen's terms: "Have you had credit for many years, or for a short time?"

- *Payment History* – "Do you have any payments later than 30 days?"

- *Credit Card Balances* – "How many different accounts do you have? How much do you owe?"

- *Requests for Credit* – "How many times have you had your credit checked for a loan?"

FICO scores would go a bit further, asking the previous questions plus wanting to know your debt-to-income ratio. FICO scores are the most common metric to determine your risk, as it is used in more than 90% of all credit decisions for lenders. Whether you're evaluating your FICO or common scores from known credit agencies, these scores are the equivalent to your personal stat sheet. Like a premier athlete, your job is to have a LeBron James credit score. How are you able to accomplish this, you ask? The answer is heavily dependent on your financial knowledge, time, and diligence.

Personal credit: The road to 800

The road to 800 can seem like a tricky one. However, all you really ever need is a 720 credit score or higher. It's almost like getting a car; all you really need are wheels to get you from point A to point B, but we salivate over a Ferrari or Lamborghini. Having the highest credit score possible just looks so much better. It's also a great conversation starter and creates an impression. As we are in the spirit of getting our credit scores to platinum status, let's see how we could increase ours to get or stay there by understanding the credit scoring algorithm.

*Photo credit: Student loan hero

Payment history

We should first follow the **35/30/15/10/10** model. Since 35% of your score is dependent on payment history, missing a single payment, even if you're closing the account based on a sale, could spell doom to your credit score. However, contrary to popular financial judgment, you aren't a loser if you fall behind on a payment. There are many resources out there that offer services that can help wipe out derogatory remarks from late and missed payments on your credit score. The real problem is the lack of access we have to this help. Sometimes the answer is right in front of you. No, really, right in front of you. You're reading it (*shameless plug, might I add*). There are many credit repair services such as Credit Karma, amongst others, that for a few bucks could help you clear these derogatory remarks and boost your credit score. It's funny because if it works, 35% of your credit score will be positively affected and boost your credit score substantially.

Utilization

The next number, 30, comes from the fact that 30% of your credit score is based on the amount of credit you are using, often referred to as a utilization rate. Utilizing a high percentage of your available credit means you're close to maxing out your credit cards, which can have a negative impact on your FICO score. It does not matter if you have a credit card that gives you unlimited access to large amounts of credit. If you want to be in good standing, you should aim to keep your utilization under 30%. Hard to accomplish if the only access to capital that you have is through the use of credit. This is why credit should be used strategically and with care.

Length of credit

Let's look at the next number: 15% of your score is your length of credit history. This one is harder to control because the length of your credit accounts is directly related to how much time you've had the credit open. In other words, How long have your credit accounts been open? The longer the years, the better it will be to have a positive score in this area. Although the credit bureaus determine this to have a 15% impact in your credit score, having a solid history can in fact boost your credit score exponentially. So, the longer you have your revolving credit, the better.

Credit mix

If you want to be in good standing and boost your credit score even higher, then you have to have a proper mix of credit.

The credit *mix* consists of the following:

➢ ***Revolving accounts*** - Credit cards

➢ ***Installment accounts*** – Mortgage, car loans, and student loans

Whether you like it or not, you have to have that proper mix of credit cards and other installment loans, especially if you want to get into the 700s and beyond.

New Credit

Lastly comes new credit. Although having a small impact (10%), opening too many or too little credit lines could significantly impact your score. Confused? Welcome to the complex world of FICO credit scoring. The goal is to show that you are taking on new credit as needed, not out of desperation or the urge to access new credit in order to obtain capital. However, the fear of taking on new credit can often be excessive and unnecessary. Since this category, of new credit, accounts for just 10 percent of a borrower's overall FICO score, you should probably focus on improving other aspects of your behavior rather than worrying about opening new accounts.

Credit Scoring HACK - (Piggy Backing)

Establishing great personal credit is essential to building wealth in America. But how are people able to access the capital needed to catapult themselves out of poverty with bad credit? Well, did you know that you can have yourself added to someone else's credit profile, meaning her credit card accounts, and within 30 to 45 days, you would immediately adopt the entire history of that account? If you didn't, well, you're welcome! I just revealed a credit *hack* for you.

If you needed good credit to, let's say, buy a house, a car, or get access to capital via a loan, but you have been suffering with bad personal credit, then this strategy would apply to you. It's known as the *Authorized User* strategy or *Piggy Backing*. It's simple, you can approach a friend or family member who has established a great credit relationship with a credit card provider, and have him make the request to the creditor to add you on their credit card as an *Authorized User*. In doing so, the primary account holder will NOT be penalized or have their credit scores negatively impacted by adding you; however, their positive credit will show up on yours! It's a win-win scenario.

An authorized user is *different* from a cosigner because at any time, the primary account holder can remove you from her account. A cosigner cannot be removed until the account is paid in full. I highly discourage anyone from being a cosigner on any loan. I don't care if it's your spouse or your grandmother. Cosigning is suicide. But having or being an authorized user is a credit hack that could allow you to build credit without putting someone else's score in jeopardy.

Side note: The best possible accounts to be added to or to add someone else as an *authorize user*, is an account that actually reports to the credit bureaus. You can simply find this out by asking the credit card company if they report to the bureaus. If they say yes, then that's the account for you. If they say no, then simply try a credit card account that does report. Always remember that the authorized user does not have to have access to spend money on the account; it's only about adopting the primary holder's history.

Here are three things to consider to make this tool work:

1. The account has to *report* to the three credit bureaus

2. You have to only have a *positive* account history

3. Large credit limit of at least *$5,000*

4. Account has to be *paid on time* with a *low balance*

This is a very savvy, yet practical technique that is a sure way to increase your, or someone you love's, credit instantly and exponentially!

Another credit hack: This hack only works when the statement date on your credit card is coming up. Paying down your balance *in the days before* it gets reported to the credit bureaus could give your scores a boost.

Bad Credit . . . meet Business Credit

It seems like there is a ton of information out there regarding personal credit. However, when it comes to business credit . . . crickets! There is still hope for you to access credit and revitalize your negative experience with credit, while setting you on a different path of getting access to capital altogether. Yes, I am talking about business credit! But, can business credit really be an alternative to bad personal credit? The answer is heavily dependent upon your financial savviness, business acumen, and how well you receive what I am about to reveal. Let us take a look.

Business credit is very similar to personal credit in that it has to be in great standing in order to get access to capital to qualify for loans, lower interest rates, and increase cash flow. Just like with personal credit, the earlier you start to build it, the better. Time is an asset as it relates to building both personal and business credit scores. You don't want to wait until you are shopping for a car or a house to start building business credit. This should be done when you have no reason to buy anything. So, preparation is key.

There are many benefits in looking towards business credit as a solution to a bad credit score. These benefits include:

1. **Your *business credit* account has NO effect on your *personal credit*** – For example, if you have a 500 personal credit score, but a great business credit score, you can still get access to capital if you use your business credit to do so.

2. **Your personal credit will not take a hit on a business credit check** – *Because business credit and personal credit are kept separate, your personal credit will not be hit if you*

decide to shop for a loan on your business credit. In other words, you leverage your business credit to get the money while your personal credit remains untouched.

There is hope after all. Exciting news, right!? Your next inclination is probably to wonder how to get started. Well, there are eight simple, but effective steps to help you build excellent business credit.

<u>These steps are:</u>

1. ***Choose a business structure:*** *T*he first and obvious step that you should take is setting up a business entity. Whether you decide to use a C-corp, S-corp, LLC, or other entity, this will allow you to start the process of building your business credit.

2. ***Get an Employer ID number (EIN):*** Think of this number as your business social security number. By establishing an EIN, you will be able to use it to open up a bank account, get a credit card, and file taxes under this number.

3. ***Get a DUNS number:*** Ah! This step is extremely critical. Your company D-U-N-S number is simply your credit profile, you know, the one you see for your personal credit score on Credit Karma. Similar to Credit Karma, the most popular place to check to access your DUNS number would be Dun & Bradstreet. Also, be sure to contact Experian business to be added to their business credit monitoring system as well.

4. ***Update your business information:*** Make sure your company stays current with the myriad amount of regulations, annual payments, and company information needed in order to ensure a solid score.

5. ***Pay on time or early:*** Pretty straightforward. Any debt or vendor payments that you incur must be paid on time and regularly. Getting a DUNS number will allow you to report every payment and transaction made on your end to help boost your business credit score.

6. ***Get vendor references:*** If you've established a relationship with a vendor or cc company that know you on a first-name basis, obtaining a reference from them could also help your business credit score increase.

7. ***Monitor your score:*** Any new information such as late payments, liens, judgments, or bankruptcies can negatively affect your credit score. So frequently checking up could help you stay on top of any movements on your score and keep you on top of your credit.

8. ***Keep inquires low:*** Similar to your personal credit score, too many inquiries could negatively affect your business credit. An inquiry is simply when a company runs your credit in order to determine if you can be trusted with a loan or any other terms relating to business.

Interestingly enough, many of us have absolutely no clue that there is another, alternative way to build credit outside of personal credit. It almost seems as if the popular financial rhetoric that we're receiving is deliberately hiding loopholes like the ones mentioned previously. No worries, this is where I come in. I will reveal this esoteric information that is kept hidden in plain sight from the masses, and give it to you in a way that is easy to digest and comprehend. In the end, having access to information is key. Building your business credit is another way to remedy bad or declining personal credit.

Your personal income statement is also credit

I cannot stress this enough—ownership is a wealth trap repellant—and now I can tell you that ownership is also a bad credit repellant. In my case, when I purchased my first investment property, it was my tenants' money that helped to build my credit score. The rent coming in from them served as sort of a *bond* and granted a consistent monthly payment. Every year that passed, the rent was never raised, so my turnover rate would be low and the tenant would be able to make the payments on time and consistently. By not raising the rents, I was playing chess with my personal credit. By doing so, the tenant was forced to stay, because it would cost them more to leave and rent elsewhere; the risk on my end was low, due to the low mortgage that I would have to pay if the tenant would leave. And if the tenant did decide to leave, I would raise the rent to just under market value once again and get another tenant two weeks later. Knocking on wood, I have never made a mortgage payment to date. My tenants are responsible for increasing my personal and business credit. Banks also see this and, as a result, are happy to finance my next property. This is because my personal income statement reveals my true value and creditworthiness.

In the end, there are loopholes that come with popular financial rhetoric. This information is spewed by popular financial advisors, coaches, and the media, but there is one thing that they are consistently missing. Everyone's situations and motivations are different. This also applies to credit scores and personal income statements. Some of this hidden information goes to only the 1% who benefit from receiving financial information that is tailored to them. This is the information of opportunity, calculated risk, leveraging OPM & OPT, developing high emotional intelligence, and most importantly, *ownership*. The financial nobu-like type of information designed for the wealthy. The masses, however, are only offered financial fast food designed to keep us trapped in the rat race. It's now time to crack down on this information and reimagine what authentic and tailored financial information looks like.

CHAPTER 7

GoFundMe is not Life Insurance

Allow me to repeat: GoFundMe is not life insurance. People insure their homes, their cars, cell phones, and even pets. But what is the most important thing in your life? Most wouldn't hesitate to answer: family. Yet so many of us are uninsured. The cost to protect you and your family can be no more than 50 cents per day, and can ensure a positive economic outlook for your family in the event of a tragedy. Think about how much we spend per day on our vices, whether that be coffee, or taking an Uber or Lyft down the street when we can walk. The reality is, whether it be through a trust, or insurance, we could allocate this money to insure our families are protected financially.

TAX Yourself first

Part of planning is ensuring that you have the means to do so. Having a financial or estate plan is no different. You want to ensure that you are setting yourself up to enjoy the financial fruits of your labor as well as pass it on for your kids to enjoy as well. What I'd start to do first instead of jumping into insurance, assets, and setting up trusts, wills, and other forms of asset protection, I like to test how disciplined I am. In order to test my ability to not overextend myself, I tax myself first. Every time I get paid or get access to capital, I immediately pay myself before I pay for anything else. The funds can then be allocated to various sources, including life insurance policies. You don't have to invest your entire income or nest egg into life insurance policies, as you will see with other strategies that I reveal, but getting started by having the means to invest in whole life or term policies will require that you have money to spend on these vehicles in the first place. I'm sure you can find many different opinions related to term policies versus whole life, but one thing is for certain—if anything happens to you, your family will be safe. My grandfather used to say, "A true man can support his kids and grandkids, even in death." This is how you do can do this.

The difference between a *will* and *"living"* revocable trust.

You are probably wondering what the hell is a living revocable trust, and why you would need a living revocable trust when there are wills. Well, allow me to explain why. First of all, a will is simply a piece of paper that states where your assets are to go upon your death. For example, let's say your mother owns a house in the state of California worth $500,000, but she has little to no equity in the property. She has a will that says you get the house upon her death. All you have left after her death is this piece of paper called a will, stating that you are to get the property. But the title of the property is in her name, and she's not alive to sign the title to you! So now you have to hire a lawyer (expensive) to take this paper down to probate court. The judge will have to read the letter and validate the will, and this process takes almost a year! Tie that in with the expense from the lawyer and statutory probate fees, and you have the ingredients for a sale of the house in order to pay for the fees accrued. There goes your generational wealth.

What could your mother have done to avoid this from occurring? Simple. She could have taken steps while alive to create what is known as a living revocable trust. A living revocable trust is easy to comprehend:

Living: Taking steps to transfer title while living (*or alive*)
Revocable: She could change it anytime
Trust: The name of the document

Your parent takes the steps, while alive, to transfer the title of the house from her name, into a trust. Your parent will be the trustor (the one who created it), and the trustee (the one who gets to make all of the decisions). The house is also held for your parent's benefit while she is alive, and when your parent dies you become the successor beneficiary, allowing the house to be immediately transferred to you without the additional time and cost.

The Dynasty Trust

Ah! I believe this is a trust that is kept from the masses for a reason and I will share why. Allow me to ask you the following questions:

- Do you want to know why the rich really get richer?

- Do you want protection for your son or daughter in the event they get divorced?

- Do you want your money to last not just one generation, but multiple generations?

- Do you want to protect this wealth from lawsuits?

- Do you want to avoid the estate tax altogether?

If so, you want to know what a dynasty trust is and why you need this particular trust over a regular trust. Here is why you will find this interesting. . . . Let's say you have a child who is terrible with money, or in the process of getting married to someone who is, and part of you knows that the inheritance you are planning to give to your child will not last. All you have to do to prevent this is create a dynasty trust. This is a document that protects your estate on many levels after you die.

Here's how it works:

You put your assets into a regular trust, and upon your death, instead of everything going outright to your child, which is the way you most likely have it set up now, your regular trust feeds what you're giving to your child into a dynasty trust. The dynasty trust lives well beyond you and states that your child may not turn these assets over to the husband or wife. In other words, it goes directly to your grandchildren, not the spouses or husbands of your child(ren). Think about it, what if your child gets a divorce, or is married to someone who's only been in the picture for a few days (Khloé and Lamar), and then you die. In a trust, the husband has the opportunity to get access to the money. In a dynasty trust, he doesn't.

Simply put, a dynasty trust says no to your child's spouse. The assets are simply and only available for the benefit of your child, and the children of your child. So if you want protection for the possibility if your child gets a divorce, or protection from lawsuits, if you want the estate tax savings, or even to make sure that the money gets to the grandchildren and lasts more than one generation, then you need a dynasty trust!

Note: Always consult with an attorney to get specifics and a more thorough insight according to YOUR situation. Remember, everybody's situation is different.

Unified credit – Escape the estate tax?

People often ask me if they can give money away without being taxed. The answer is YES! If you're fortunate enough to have more than $675,000, or $5 million, but want to escape the estate tax upon death, then I have the perfect solution for you! If you haven't heard of a loophole known as the unified tax credit, I advise you to pay attention to what I am about to reveal. This, I believe, could possibly be an estate tax loophole commonly used and practiced among the elite, but kept out of popular financial planning and advice for the masses.

You can make gifts at $14,000 or more per year to any of your children or grandchildren. That's right! You can gift as many people as you'd like $14,000 or more per year. Now here is the kicker. Remember the exemption amount is up to $675,000, so if you have an estate less than this amount, you can gift it all without being taxed on any of the amount given. There are even some cases where you can gift up to $5.75 million through this exclusion, and not be taxed federally at all! This loophole is called the unified tax credit and is one of the many strategies used among the wealthy to avoid the estate tax.

Now the only thing to look out for is the taxes the inheritance will have to pay on any *gains* that are incurred by the beneficiary. In other words, if you give your child $50,000, and your child invests this money and makes an extra $8,000, your child will only be subjected to pay taxes on the $8,000. There is no step-up in basis, which is beyond the scope of this topic. However, it would be worse if the beneficiary inherits your estate after you pass on. The inheritor of the estate, or beneficiary, would still pay taxes on any profit or gain from the principal, and unlike the unified credit, the estate would even be taxed. Double taxation vs. no taxes; which would you choose?

Wealth Insurance

Anytime a society has printed fiat currency, whether it be Germany, Venezuela, or Zimbabwe, it hasn't gone well. There were people within these countries who had a great deal of fiat currency to leave for their children, but failed to seek out insurance on their money. When the nation's monetary system imploded, so did these individuals' money. This was a valuable lesson in protecting your currency with money. So my question to you is: What is the point in ensuring your legacy if you aren't insuring your money? How does someone get insurance against a currency, like the U.S. dollar, that is 100% promised to never fail? Simple—you ensure it with God's money, gold and silver. Gold, atomic number 79, and Silver, atomic number 47, was here before humanity, and will be here even after the cockroaches have all died. They have been a consistent and proven barometer of any fiat currency to have ever existed, and like real estate, are a hedge against inflation. There is a reason why the price of gold has increased as more currency has been printed. There is a limited supply of gold and silver and is widely utilized in almost everything we use in modern society today. This is why not adding physical gold and silver could be like not getting life insurance on your money. No, I am not pointing to (exchange traded funds) ETF gold and silver, like the gld and the slv, although you could possibly profit from speculation. I am talking about something you can hug at night. Physical base metals like gold and silver will not make you rich, but they will almost certainly preserve your wealth. If you are looking to jump in on the gold and silver hype and a get-rich-quick scheme, then this section may not be for you. However, if you are interested in insuring your money, or if you're worried about hyper-inflation ensuing because of the massive printing our central bank has been doing, then physical gold and silver may be an option for you. It will help you sleep better at night knowing that, in a way, you have both ends covered.

This information, although commonly known, is rarely practiced or discussed in mainstream financial education spheres. My job is to equip you with the knowledge unknown to the masses in order to ensure your financial legacy remains intact and vibrant. Instead of waiting until it is too late to give to the next generation, you are able to avoid any possible tax liability or probate trouble by leveraging these loopholes to share your wealth both safely and legally.

CHAPTER 8

ALL BUSINESS

Odds are, you probably won't become the next billionaire running a business or selling a product or service. A lot of people have some crazy expectations when it comes to being an entrepreneur or a business owner. I know we live in a time where if you're not making *a million dollars*, you are considered a loser or invaluable according to your peers. But look at it this way, earning a thousand dollars or more a month in passive income for not doing any work (outside of the initial effort needed to create the income stream) isn't bad at all. Especially if you don't have to be in a major city like New York in order to do so! Are you interested in creating a stream of revenue to offset any debt burdens in your life? Or simply put, are you interested in creating true freedom for yourself and live your best life? Well, it's time to learn from the experiences and examples that I will share with you.

In a gold rush, don't go digging for gold . . .

Instead, sell shovels.

BUSINESSES are not hobbies

The only reason for a business to exist in the first place is to solve a problem or a need. You would think something so simple would be obvious, right!? Unfortunately, it isn't. We sometimes fall victim to the whole "find your passion, or follow your dreams" advice. Your passion or dreams are only engines to move the wheels of adding true value in the world. You still need to identify a problem and find a *market fit* for your product or service. Here's an example: If there are 1,000,000 trainers all doing what they love, but only 50 people demand to be trained, do you think passion will pay the bills? I think not. The genesis of business creation is to find an unfilled niche and add value or solve a problem or need. You cannot create a market that doesn't want to exist. It's a simple concept; however, business is far from simple. Unless you are leveraging a franchise or preexisting business, it is quite challenging to educate the consumer, let alone have her buy in, if the consumer is used to social norms. This may actually prove that you are creating a need rather than actually identifying one. Both may work, but one will be harder to convert your targeted audience to than the other. Always remember, if your business is not ready to receive full-time attention, then the money won't be either.

Question: *Interested in building a technology start-up?*

1. To build a great and sustainable company, you first need to:

2. Think about the market and what it wants.

3. Turn a great idea into a great product.

4. Talk to your customers/users.

5. Find a small group of users and make them love your product.

6. Make it simple!

This is the only way to organic growth and leverage on your end. A great product that does one thing extremely well is the secret to long-term growth hacking. Always remember, over the long run, great but simple products win. Just look at Apple.

Owning your platform

I want you to think about where and how you are building your business, brand, or relationships. Can someone, whether it be a person, entity, or company, slip the rug from under you or your business at any moment, and cause you to lose all of your money, customers, or fame? If that is the case, then you are not owning your platform. Owning your platform is like the land on which you are building your business, brand, or relationships on. If 100% of your product's sales, income, or brand is coming from one channel, then one algorithm change, one bad argument with your boss, one bad hit on your reputation, can immediately propel you from a hero, to a zero, overnight! And you did absolutely nothing wrong! Just look at all of the Vine and Myspace influencers, or your favorite entertainers who are no longer relevant in society's viewpoint. This is why third-party platforms, or middlemen, can be troublesome if you are solely dependent on them individually. The solution is to own your platform and leverage as many intermediaries as you can. Don't get stuck depending on one platform to support you, whether it be selling stuff on Amazon, working at a corporation, signing on to a record label, or seeking out traditional education. These institutions and infrastructures, with a stroke of a pen, can abandon their model, or not work for you, leaving you holding the bag. The point here is risk. Your goal should be to minimize risk by maximizing platforms available to you. This is how you own your platform.

Get to scale

Question: Does your product exist, even if you didn't? If not, you must learn and understand the concept of getting to scale. Ultimately, your product or service must stand alone without your connection to it. Time-honored businesses are usually involved in the act of creation and can exist and sell independent of any one person being around. This is why we hear of institutions or multinational corporations still existing even after the founder has passed on. Scale builds on time, meaning that you are replicating the difficulty in whatever you solved. An example of this would be if you're building out a solution that solves a problem, let's say, in the restaurant space. Your solution might take 5 to 6 months to build. However, the initial time building this software would have absolutely no correlation with the amount of money and value that will come as a result of it. By scaling, you can make 50 to 100 times the profit, without 50 to 100 times the work. The goal is to get to scale and expand your profits, without expanding your work. This is what separates the mom-and-pop businesses from the multinational ones. Scalability.

Building a brand

Whenever you're building a brand, whether it be for a company, book, product, or service, you must first know the following:

1. Who are you?

2. What do you represent?

3. What do you believe in?

4. How do you desire to make someone feel?

The reason you have to ask yourself these questions, is because you have to be willing to stick to it at all costs and under all circumstances. If you want to have a strong brand for the long term, you have to stand for it, even if people don't agree or support you or the vision. Eventually they will come around, and if not, the right people for you will. Even more, if you're just starting out, but don't know where and how to begin, simply model what has been done before. Compare the branding approach to a company, brand, business, or style that you like. Ask yourself the following questions:

- What is your favorite brand/company?

- Why do you like this brand/company?

- What is the aspirational concept, or movement, behind this company that compels you?

- If you could describe it in one word, what would that word be?

I like the brand Versace. Maybe not so much for its clothes; although I would definitely wear a good pair of boxers. I like the line for how it was able to distinguish itself as a premium brand for the elite. I think the ultimate form of branding comes from . . . well, let me ask you. What comes to mind when you hear Versace in Miami? If you said the Versace mansion, you get where I am going with this. This is the power of branding that comes from emotion, memory, and culture. The Versace mansion is indicative of a lifestyle. The clothing line is designed to reflect that approach. If my brand, product, or lifestyle were to emulate anything, it would be Versace. Now, what would I have to do in order for that to happen? If I want to build a brand similar to Versace, then all of my visuals would have to reflect a rich and wealthy lifestyle. It wouldn't matter if it was a book, tech product, small business, or intellectual property, everything that I should associate a brand with should be luxurious. You have to do this 24 hours a day, 7 days a week. You can also have influencers or celebrities endorse your brand as well. This is how you establish a brand: consistency, reinforcement, and influence.

You only need to be right once

That's right! You only have to be right once to be considered a success. Don't believe me? Let's take a look at people who have:

1. ***Thomas Edison** failed 10,000 times before perfecting the lightbulb.*

2. ***Mark Zuckerberg** had Facebook registered as an LLC in Florida and almost sabotaged his ability to raise capital.*

3. *Reid Hoffman before co-founding LinkedIn and investing in big names like PayPal and Airbnb, created Social Net, an online dating and social networking site that ultimately failed.*

4. *Cathy Hughes, the founder of TV One, attributed her success from learning from her constant failures and the 1,000 no's she received.*

The way to be successful in business, as in all other aspects of life, is to never give up. This does not mean that, if something is not working, you shouldn't pivot or change the target. What I mean is, you shouldn't allow quitting to be a part of your vocabulary. If, in your perspective, you feel like you failed, simply identify and reflect on what you could have done better and do it. It doesn't matter if you are working on a different product or rebranding; the goal is to keep building until you get it right! Now if 10 things fall through, but that one idea works, it is imperative that you exploit what's working and maximize the result of it. Because that exponential growth never lasts forever. It eventually levels off or runs dry. The goal is to be right once, identify it, maximize the success, and preserve the fruits from it.

Raising Capital

Some people would say that the term *raising capital* isn't a viable option, and is more of a tasteful form of begging than creatively receiving. Others would consider it a necessity in the quest to accessing the capital needed to grow, buy, or expand in any endeavor. Either way, raising capital is here to stay and is commonly practiced in business.

Real Estate

Interested in ownership in real estate, but don't have the funds you need to get started? If you are not already aware, there are many ways to own property without going through a traditional bank. There are also specific loopholes that will allow you to secure a mortgage on an investment property for 5% to 35% down if you lack the sufficient credit or ownership history. Now I know you're wondering, *Where in the hell am I going to come up with a 35% down payment on an investment property?* Simple. Raise enough capital that will cover the down payment, whether it be 5% or 35%. There are tons of ways, such as:

Group economics - raising money from friends and family.

Starting a Real Estate Investment Trust (R.E.I.T.) – pool a group of investors who put money in to invest in real estate projects in exchange for profit sharing of your business.

Starting a Real Estate Fund: This requires more regulatory hurdles, but is a great way to access the power of communities to pool money in to increase your capital reserves required to compete with hedge funds at auction houses.

Believe it or not, people need to live, regardless of what state you are in. As long as there are jobs, there will be people. Places like North Carolina, Delaware, Texas, Oklahoma City are ideal for first-time investors looking to get in the game. But what's the alternative if you lack the cash? Raising capital by crowdfunding, or partnering with someone, can be the solution to your initial financial hurdle. It's easier said than done, but there is a way to do it. You'd be surprised how much money you, your family, or peers would stumble on for trips, unwarranted expenses, bond and bails, and even for an education for a loved one.

Technology

Now there are popular networks to tap into in order to get access to the necessary capital you need to grow your business. Odds are, you've probably heard of incubators, angel investors, and even venture capitalists. In my opinion, although these are viable resources to tap into to grow your business, they are innovation traps. The reason is because this option forces you to wait on the major players to see the value in your idea, and more often than not comes with strings attached to the terms on any offer that you get. Why not start with crowdfunding, or raising money within your inner network first? I am not talking about an astronomical number, nor am I talking about just asking your parents for 40K (that they may not even have) like Mitt Romney would suggest. What I am referring to is leveraging community and online platforms to share your initiatives. If you are an active member in your school, non-profit, church, or any other socially driven enterprise, then you could collaborate with them and host community events that expose people to your product or service. By utilizing technology financing, like Indiegogo and others, you are able to raise capital on site. By following this strategy, it gives people the opportunity to see and feel the product, and they will be more likely to invest.

The truth is, this strategy can in fact be applied to any idea or business that you're looking to have funded. I am not saying that you need to avoid incubators and angels like a plague. I am simply pointing to other creative ways that you can tap into, if you are looking for cash to grow your business. When you start to think creatively, then you will never feel like there is only one way to get the necessary access to capital.

Have other creative ways and industry to raise money? Jot them down here:

_____

_____

_____

_____

_____

_____

_____

_____

What the media doesn't share about business

Pursuing a business is a very noble thing to do, but only for a fraction of a percentage of people reading this. You really know if you're an entrepreneur or built for business if you have a burning desire to want to be independent, and if you think money buys freedom. It doesn't mean that your life is easier as an entrepreneur or business owner; in fact, you have to make a ton of sacrifices and experience failures on the road to success. Starting down the path of entrepreneurship means that you have to sacrifice a lot for the period that you're growing or building your business, and not everyone wants to do that. Whether you're an employee, seeking to transition to entre-preneurship, or someone who has no choice but to test the waters, then I recommend you start down this path and be as resourceful as possible. This means you should aim to not sink all of your capital into any endeavor that you're starting until you find product market fit and start producing revenue. Start down that path, and if it's too much of a sacrifice, you can revert right back to being an employee like nothing happened. This is why it is sometimes best to be broke or act broke in your pursuit to building your business or investing for that matter. That way you don't blow it all up and you can recover if everything implodes.

CHAPTER 9
PROFIT LIKE A BIG WIG

Welcome back! Nice to see you are interested in learning more from the graduate school of capitalism and wealth. This is information that is rarely given, if at all, in business schools and even MBA programs. That is because this esoteric insight is taught through experience and real-world application. Profiting like the big wig that you are is about teaching you what real entrepreneurship and wealth creation means, which is the creation of exponential value even with little or no resources, and how to do it. For the sake of this chapter, we will avoid the mainstream version of what capitalism is, because they often confuse real capitalism with *managerial capitalism*, or controlling other people's time and money.

There is a difference between equity and money

Allow me to explain; there is a difference between equity and money as it relates to business! The exorbitant difference lies in the return you get from betting on yourself in the long term, versus only getting upfront money or a paycheck. Whether it be your time, money, risk tolerance, or effort, having an equity mind-set will enable you to build, not only a giant income, but also intergenerational wealth, or wealth that you can pass down. Having an equity mind-set will allow you to identify your value, forcing you to not settle for anything less than the best. Philosophically speaking, deciding between having an equity vs. money mentality, is heavily tied to how you see yourself. Society and the workforce often have a way of telling you what your value is, and hoping—no, expecting—that you agree to their terms and assessment of you. It's as if you are a number, who has no bargaining power in a market that converts people to settle every day. An equity mind-set is the way to demand your worth, without having the anxiety of losing the thing you're dependent upon. Your job can fire you, a corporation you're representing can sever ties at any moment if it's in their interest, and someone can choose not to bring you in based on social factors. Equity and ownership could and will always soften this blow.

There is substantial discomfort and work required from the former. However, an equity mind-set individual is not here to just represent the company they work for, or be an affiliate of something. No, the equity mind-set wants to be partner, have control of their integrity, spearhead social responsibility, and most importantly retain ownership in what they're doing. Class B shareholders, or corporate stock plans won't cut it. You can be an intreprenuer, working for someone, or an entrepreneur with no resources available, and have this mind-set. The goal is to create enough leverage and value add, so that you can negotiate on your terms. Which mind-set do you have?

Predict the future

I love attempting to predict the future, which I have found many millionaires and billionaires like to do as well. How do you predict the future, you ask? It's actually quite simple; look at history. I'm sure many of you have heard the saying, "History doesn't necessarily repeat, but it often rhymes," and this couldn't be any closer to the truth. That is why we always witness cycles of life. Whether financial, relationship, health, and spiritual cycles, there are always stages of corrections and growth. The way to profit like a big wig is to understand these cycles in our economy. There are many different cycles, but the main ones to pay attention to are the boom and bust cycles and human behavior. If you understand that irrational exuberance has historically led to economic meltdowns, you are better prepared to predict what will happen the next time you identify another phase of irrational exuberance. Predicting the future means identifying the mistakes made in the past. This is the information that wealthy and successful investors are keen to know. They understand the philosophy and psychology of human behavior. That is why many of the people running our monetary system have degrees in psychology to go along with their MBAs. Predicting the future for them is anticipating human behavior and macroeconomic trends within society. And if you understand this along with the human mind, it leaves nothing to chance.

Multiple Copies of the Original Form

The successful and erudite entrepreneur knows that the remedy of generating an infinite return starts with creating value and replicating this value production AT SCALE. Whether you're starting a business, creating a product or service, leveraging your money or even investing, the principles of money apply the same way. So how do you begin to produce value with no money or resources?

Simple! Become your own version of the *federal reserve*.

For those of you who don't know who or what the *federal reserve* is, I have thoroughly explained the federal reserve, or "the fed," perfectly in my previous book, *Financial Freedom: My Only Hope*. Simply put, the fed is a privately held organization, who has this unique ability to issue or print the nation's currency out of thin air and control it through inflation. Now, when I make the correlation between the federal reserve and yourself, what I am saying is, you can create value out of nothing.

You can create value out of nothing through:

- *Entrepreneurship*

- *Real Estate*

- *Investing*

- *Technology*

- *Writing*

- *Teaching*

- *Entertaining*

- *Networking*

- *Online platforms (YouTube, Social Media, Website/Blog)*

Think   of   some   other   ways: ————————————,
————————————, ————————————,

Multiple copies of my first app

In my experience with applying this method, I was able to create exponential value out of nothing simply by creating a technology product, in this case a mobile application, and then distributing it exponentially (through the use of the App Store, a major mobile application distributor), to different people around the world who wanted to experience playing the gaming app. The first version of my mobile application started in a small niche, but eventually evolved in market size. Through applying this mind-set, I was able to create this app from an idea in my mind and distribute thousands of copies from only one initial effort.

Multiple copies of my books

Why have all of this inherent knowledge and information burning a hole in your mind, if you are going to keep it to yourself? What if I told you that there are people in the world who need what you have to offer? Even better, what if I told you that, with just some initial effort, you could create a form of value added for your audience and monetize it by printing multiple copies of your original work? Yes! You can monetize what I call your intellectual property. This is anything that is intrinsic and requires little to no physical labor on your end.

You can *monetize* your intellectual property related to the following:

- Thoughts

- Knowledge on a particular subject

- Expertise

- Wisdom/Experience

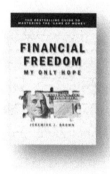

In my experience, writing a book started as a way of organizing my thoughts and business strategies, but soon transformed into something much more valuable. Producing literature became a form of being my own version of the fed. Although writing books required a substantial amount of focus, time, work, and effort, the initial sacrifice would yield a return far greater than the effort. Outside of the obvious monetary gain, I was able to foster new relationships, build a loyal following, and affect lives for the better. I am able to create something that will last well beyond my years, adding value and monetizing a product with an infinite return on my time. This form of value creation is key.

Money is seen with your mind, not with your eyes.

—Jeremiah Brown

Ultimately, in order to achieve this type of value creation, you have to think like the federal reserve. Creativity, wisdom (often from failure), and personal cultivation is needed in order to accomplish this form of income and wealth building.

Cash-strapped investing

Looking to profit like a big wig, but are financially strapped? You may want to pay attention to this section closely. New real estate investors or those who have no money and bad credit can utilize this strategy to profit like a seasoned investor. The most successful real estate investors have found that using other people's money (OPM) frees up their cash to invest in even more! Want to know how? Well, here are some of the different ways they are able to invest in real estate without putting any money down.

1. ***Hard money or private lenders:*** *Through the help of a hard money lender, you could finance any real estate deal without having to put up that 10% to 20% down payment, like you would through a bank. These types of lenders can be anyone, from your friend, to a business, or even your parent, who has access to capital, and is willing to lend out on a good property or deal. Here is the best part; the investors get to create their own terms on the loan. What's the benefit? A more lenient qualification process, and the ability to put less money down and leverage some of the cash flow of the property to pay the lender back. The interest rates may be high, so make sure your property is cash flowing more than the monthly loan amount. So, whenever faced with that "I'm broke, or I have bad credit" dilemma, know that there is this option to getting into real estate.*

2. ***Wholesaling****: This is another interesting way to get into real estate without having a high credit score or large sums of money. Here's how it works:*

   ➤ Find a discounted property

   ➤ Put property under contract

   ➤ Assign the contract to a buyer

   ➤ Charge a finder's fee from 10% to 15% of the sale

   ➤ Rinse and repeat

It's almost the equivalent to being a real estate agent without going through the process of getting all of the qualifications. With this strategy you can be a broker without having a broker's license. Though this process may appear simple and straightforward, you will need to either be a part of a network or use websites that have a database of investors and properties already, in order to facilitate these deals.

3. **Home equity:** *If you already own a property, or inherited a property from a loved one, then using your home's equity is a way to invest in more real estate without having to use all of your capital. You can use a cash out refinance, where you simply get cash with your new loan, and use that cash to purchase an investment property under an LLC that you create.*

4. **Lease option agreement:** *The lease option or master lease agreement allows you to acquire a property, without initially taking ownership. Similar to an option on a stock, you are simply signing an option to buy the property for a specific price in the future. In return, the investor rents the property to you for the period in which you agree to. So if you agree to a 5, 10, 20, or 30-year lease option, that means you will pay the owner the full amount in the said years, and the owner is renting the property to you until it is paid off. Once you pay it off, or the lease option ends, you own the property. This is great because if you sign a lease option on, lets say the Empire State Building for 30 years, by the time the 30 years come, the appreciation from the building alone will be enough to pay off the balance of the lease option. You will also be able to collect rents from the Empire State Building to pay the owner his monthly check. So, basically, with this strategy, you own the Empire State Building with no money down and leverage the cash flow from it to pay the investor until it's times for you to take over the property. The best*

thing about this is you get all the benefits of owning the real estate. You get the tax write-off, the appreciation, and any profit from cash flow after paying the investor his monthly note for renting you the property. This scenario really happened. Look it up!

Just because you have a lack of capital or bad credit doesn't mean you are excluded from profiting like a *big-wig* investor in real estate. If you want to invest in real estate using little to none of your money at all, then identifying and practicing these strategies that I've provided will allow you to build wealth quickly and be ahead of the curve! You just need to know where to start, or how to creatively get access to capital to finance these deals and make a profit.

Commercial Real Estate Investing

So, you've acquired some cash to invest, maybe not enough to be a majority owner of your favorite professional sports team, but you would still like to test your business acumen by dipping your foot into commercial property. Why am I not surprised? I mean, you did read my last book *Financial Freedom: My Only Hope*, or have at least a fundamental understanding of how to generate wealth in real estate. So, here is my advice on how to buy a commercial property on a shoestring budget, and what to look for as you begin searching for the right deal. Ready?

Contrary to what some of the financial and real estate gurus would have you think, commercial real estate is NOT as complex as it is made out to be. You don't have to get caught up in the "bigger is better" mentality in order to earn huge profits in this space. In fact, some of the most profitable commercial deals are NOT the 500+ units or prime land you see in the center of large cities, but the ones located right in your backyard. These units or land are great because of the simple fact that you do not have to invest a ton of money in order to produce a large or infinite return on your investment. In addition, there are both *personal* and *investment* benefits to going small, as opposed to over-leveraging yourself on a huge commercial property.

The ***personal benefits*** consist of the following:

1. ***Small down payment***: *You will be dealing with modest sale prices, so you won't need a boatload of money in order to close on a small commercial deal.*

2. ***Numbers are easy to grasp***: *It will be easier to wrap your mind around the numbers on a 5- to 10-unit property, as opposed to a 3,500-unit one.*

3. ***Fewer and less costly mistakes***: *This is great if you're on a tight budget and have little capital reserves, because you are able to afford it if tenants leave or any undetected maintenance and other issues come up.*

The ***investment benefits*** consist of the following:

1. ***Less competition***: *You will be dealing mostly with less savvy (mom and pop) investors and owners, compared to larger institutions such as: R.E.I.T.S, hedge funds, and corporations who would aim for those bigger projects and deals.*

2. ***Higher "cash-on-cash" return***: *Most small investors will normally leave money on the table by not raising rents. This is because many of them are in no financial position to have high vacancy rates, so, from fear, they suppress rent prices for*

their tenants. You can easily increase your cash-on-cash by raising rents once you take over the property.

3. **Easier to wholesale**: *It is simple economics; demand is higher for smaller priced properties than larger priced ones (I only recommended this for my savvy and advanced investors).*

Whether you are already invested in commercial properties or just getting into the game for the first time, understanding both of these benefits will allow you to minimize your risk, and maximize your profits. You will begin to think like a large institution in every deal you take part in. What is so great about this opportunity, is that you will be able to do this without having large institutional capital reserves. After all, we are trying to produce an infinite return with little to none of our own money, right?

As you approach buying a commercial property, it's prudent to first understand all of the different investment assets available on the market. What are these different investment classes in regards to commercial real estate, you say? Simple; the different forms of commercial properties are:

- **Retail spaces**: Property that offers space for goods and service operating businesses. Such businesses include drug, discount, grocery, and retail stores.

- **Apartment buildings**: Five or more units are considered commercial because of the added monetary value of Net Operating Income (NOI) included in the overall value of the property.

- **Self mini storage**: Units, containers, or a space that is rented out to tenants who require storage in order to store possessions.

- **Office buildings**: *Generally classified into one of three categories—Class A, B, or C—office buildings are properties that provide rooms and space for corporations and the administrators and employees who work within them.*

- **Warehouses**: *Many companies in the logistics and manufacturing space such as Amazon, Lowes, Caterpillar, and Home Depot, all utilize this form of commercial property for their businesses.*

These are some of the many different types of commercial properties that you could purchase. Before you can buy commercial property, you first need to locate optimal financing. Here are the steps you will need to take:

1. **You must fully analyze the CRE property's income as well as its expenses:** *This is critical to understand the property's financial status and potential.*

2. *It's vital that you also **obtain insurance quotes** before you move forward with the desired property: Doing so will give you a better perspective on what the commercial property will cost you to insure.*

3. *Once you have obtained and analyzed all of the numbers, **have the property inspected:** This will insure that its condition meets regulatory standards.*

4. *Lastly, **find a lender**:* You may have to shop around in order to get the terms and rates close to what you're looking for. Make sure that the lender is qualified and has integrity. The goal here would be to secure financing for the CRE property and get the best rates and terms on the loan.

Ultimately, many of the top investors within this space are experts in two things: **a good deal** when they see it, and a **good investment property**. When it comes to finding a good deal like the top investors, you have to know and understand the market, the players, and most importantly the exit strategy. Profits in this space are made when you buy, not when you sell! As far as finding a good investment property, many of the top investors know what to look for when conducting walkthroughs or physically looking at the property. Assessing things like damage that may require repairs, or knowing how to assess risk, are important qualities you must have, if you want to find a property that is in good condition and can stay this way long term.

Here are other things to consider as you approach investing in commercial real estate:

- *Look for sellers who are motivated*

Nothing will get you a better deal than finding sellers who are motivated to sell. Nothing happens in real estate until you find a deal, which is usually accompanied by . . . you guessed it . . . a motivated seller. This is someone with a pressing reason to sell, whether financially or circumstantially motivated. The most important aspect to remember about motivated sellers is: if they aren't inclined to sell, they won't be as willing to negotiate.

- *Scouting the market/areas*

An excellent way to evaluate whether to buy commercial property is to study the local market by spending time there driving the area and touring properties. There is simply no substitute for in-person, first-hand market experience talking with neighborhood owners, and looking for vacancies. No amount of online research will give you a better handle on what really is going on.

- *Understanding the importance of relationships*

Finding and buying commercial real estate is not just about recognizing deals, finding motivated sellers, and knowing the market. At the heart of taking action is basic human communication. It's about building relationships and rapport with property owners, brokers, and other market participants so they feel comfortable talking about the good deals—and choosing to do business with you.

Side Note: You should never lease or buy commercial property without first locating and retaining experienced insiders who can guide you through the complex process. These experienced people are real estate attorneys, brokers, and Certified Public Accountants (CPA).

In the end, investing in the commercial space like the big wig that you are does not have to be at all frightening. There are many truths from popular advice regarding the risk and quarrels associated with entering into this space. However, with the right education and common sense, you will be able to think freely, independently, and take action in becoming a big wig real estate investor. The ultimate goal in this space is to have your assets pay you.

CHAPTER 10
HOW MUCH DOES A DOLLAR COST?

Ask yourself this: how is it that 50% of the population are considered financially inept, in a nation that is primarily driven on finance? How is it that one in three people who've worked their entire lives have nothing saved towards retirement? How is it that 40% of all student borrowers can't afford to make the payments on their college loans? Most of us recognize that something is terribly wrong within our economy and financial systems, yet we continue to obey the antiquated financial rhetoric spewed by the experts and media doing the opposite of what they preach. But, at what cost? If you're going to participate in this game and work to build more wealth, then the solution will be simpler than what is normally given to the 99 percenters.

Highly Educated Idiots

It's time we start changing economic philosophy if we are looking to build wealth in America. This has been one of the best times in history to not only get rich, but to build wealth. We have never in the existence of our country, seen interest rates (the cost you pay for borrowing money) so low for so long, yet all we hear from our financial media and experts is "you have to get out of debt and save, save, save." That is nuts! There is good debt, debt that allows you to purchase assets that other people are paying for, and then there is bad debt, consumer-driven debt that you have to pay back with interest on your own dime. But it takes financial education, something that is not taught in schools, to help us understand the difference. Which is probably why we have presidents, senators, and members of Congress constantly running our country into a deficit and financial crisis. Having highly intelligent idiots running the country, and failing to understand the importance of financial education, is a sure way to perpetuate the same financial mistakes from the past. This is why financial literacy is now more important than any achievement you can get in academia. With financial education, you are able to make money in any economy and ensure that you could support generations of family even after you're no longer here on this planet.

So what is the real way to make money? Is there plausible advice and solutions out there to help build wealth and invest like the wealthy? Well . . .

The real way to make money is to buy when
blood is running in the streets.

—John D. Rockefeller

Financial Advice Hidden from the 99%

Stop right here! I hope you didn't just miss the real universal answer on how to make money and build wealth in a debt-based economy. If you did, please re-read and absorb the previous quote by one of the biggest economic families in the world, the Rockefellers. John D. Rockefeller was an American oil tycoon who built one of the largest and most preeminent oil companies in the history of big business, and is the top 10 richest people of all time, lagging the great Mansa Musa, who holds the top spot as the richest person of *all time.*

So what did he mean by this quote? And why is his philosophy commonly used by the 1% and the financially savvy, but not commonly practiced in mainstream financial education? Is with- holding this information the reason why there is a huge wealth and income gap plaguing the world economy? I'll go even deeper. Is this strategy immoral and likely attributed to the reason it is kept secret from the masses?

I think the answer to these questions are heavily related to our financial vernacular and awareness on how our monetary system really works. There is no secret that another financial storm is coming. As comedian Kevin Hart would say, the way our bank account is set up exposes our economy to revolving booms and bust cycles. From lower-for-longer interest rate suppression, to corporate welfare disguised as a tax break, down to 70% of consumers spending money they don't have on things that they can't afford, you see how this economic game of financial musical chairs will come to an end, right!? Oddly enough, more than 90% of people are unaware that this is how our system works, and are unprepared for the inevitability of a downturn occurring. We are overexposed. This is why ordinary, hardworking people have lost an enormous amount of money during every economic crisis, from the dot.com and real estate bubble, back to the Great Depression. The real solution to avoiding being on the tail end of this game, is to bargain hunt for assets, like you would at CVS. Look for stocks, bonds, and real estate on sale and ensure that they are healthy assets that produce cash flow.

A lie perpetrated by the finance industry

The majority of information and financial advice consistently perpetrated by the media and finance industry is absolutely wrong. This is because there are two types of financial information in this world:

1. There is financial Information for *us, the 99%*.

2. There is financial information for *them, the 1% and .01%*.

Imagine a new Ferrari or a Lamborghini on the market with a 75% off sale. Would you not be inclined to buy the car before the sale ends and the price returns back to its original MSRP?! Well, this is the same buying strategy that the wealthy get from their financial insiders. This financial information for the .01% is to buy stocks, real estate, businesses, and now cryptocurrency when *nobody wants them*. The information given to the rich has little to do with financial data and more to do with behavioral finance and human psychology. There is a reason why many of the top economists responsible for running our monetary system never even studied finance. They instead earned credentials in the field of psychology. The financial information that is provided throughout the elite club is to buy assets when they're hated, when people are selling in fear, when there is "blood in the streets." And when is this the case? You guessed it, during bad economies and economic downturns. Instead of reacting to the media as it pertains to financial information, get your shopping list ready like the rich and get ready for a pullback. Then, buy "cash flowing" assets on sale, so that they get paid while they wait.

Two-sided financial information

The two-sided financial advice related to building wealth benefits one side of the social economic class at the expense of the other. The advice given to the 99% forces the poor and middle class to play the *game of money* as a way of survival, while the other side allows the wealthy 1% to play the game as a way of keeping score. One side is the popular and ubiquitous financial advice passed from industry leaders to the poor and middle-class wage earners. Advice such as, buy the hype (remember the Facebook IPO) and hold for dear life, or own the home you live in, and even save and pay down debt; this kind of advice I call tips for surviving, not thriving. On the other side is the advice for the wealthy. Advice such as "leverage good debt to build wealth," and "buy when the *herd*, the 99%, are selling in fear" are unconventional but effective advice given to the wealthy. Escaping the financial rat race, created from commercial financial rhetoric, requires self-education (because no one is going to learn it from mainstream advisors or the media) and a deep understanding about how money works. Above all, it comes down to a choice. Will you choose to live a life of struggle and survival, or will you live a life of abundance and gratitude? Choose wisely.

Human psychology on money

The idea that people would rather gamble than invest may be a plausible one. There is a reason why the gambling industry is a billion dollar one. Whether one is betting on a Floyd Mayweather boxing match, going to the horse race, trading cryptocurrencies in order to buying the next bitcoin, trading derivatives and options, or going to the casino, the idea (fantasy, really) is that you can double your money in a finite period of time. It is a compelling proposition. This is why people are easily deceptive to fraud, Ponzi schemes, and financial loss in the markets. It's important to know that the majority of people aren't sold on data; they're sold on emotion. They are listening to their emotions, rather than logic or getting back to the simple principles of money and business. The reality is, there is a strong instinct to want to get rich quick, even if reason dictates that the odds of gambling are stacked against us.

I too have fallen victim to this impulsive cognitive behavior. Speculating on the next big stock, investing in real estate simply because someone said the area was growing, and starting a company because the industry was popular. What I've learned is that when everybody says you should be owning something, you should be selling it, because when the bubble corrects itself, it does not touch the sides on the way down. This is why people who invest for capital gains always get crushed in the end, unless they have an enormous amount of capital reserves or are flat out lucky. You have to display an immense amount of disciple and equanimity, never allowing yourself to get caught up in the hype.

99% vs. 1 or .01?

I'm sure many of us have long been aware that the richest 1% of the population owns 1/3 of the U.S. net worth. However, there is an even smaller group at a record high, the .01%. This group of multi-billionaires tend not to only survive economic catastrophes, but come out with more wealth than they had before. Compare this to the 99% of the population—the middle class and the marginalized groups of society—and the story vastly changes. Following economic crises, they come out poorer and in more debt than before! Why is this the case? Well, the reason average Americans get hit so hard is where their wealth is derived from. Middle-class Americans have 65% of their wealth tied up in the homes they live in. However, the richest .01% of the population have their money kept in stocks, investment properties that produce cash flow, and businesses. The result? A huge and growing wealth disparity, where those in debt become dependent on the debtors to live and survive.

Today, 1 in 7 people in America live below the poverty line. For example, 14.5% of American households are considered food insecure, which simply means they are afraid that they won't be able to sustain feeding their families. All the while, sales of luxury cars, designer brands, and expensive art and jewelry and top executive pay is up. We can even talk about taxes such as carried interest loopholes, that allow billionaires in the finance industry to pay less in taxes than their secretaries. But that focus will lead us into an even deeper rabbit hole of greed and deception, which only keeps the wealth disparity ever increasing. This forces capital in the hands of the very few encouraging and spearheading a new phenomenon known as controlled capitalism. This is why the first thing people look to when starting a business or running for an election is who they are going to raise capital from. They are going to the .01% for it.

The Invisible hand

This socioeconomic divide and inequality in our society has also impacted capitalism for entrepreneurs who lack access to capital, creating a new term, controlled capitalism. This is where bankers, hedge funds, venture capital firms, and investment groups make decisions on what is and isn't considered innovative and investable. Controlled capitalism allows these financial gatekeepers to influence who gets funded. One of the issues that is always faced by new entrepreneurs is the lack of available capital to help them go into or maintain a low-income business. It's unfortunate that the vast majority of the deals and loans go to the people who don't need them. Don't believe me? Research the qualifications of getting a business loan. I am pretty sure you will have to have high revenues or assets already in place to get access to financing. Tie this with the ability to get a loan for a car, and you will see signs all over the place saying, "No down payment, no income, no problem." See the problem? It's easier to get funds necessary for consumption and speculation, than it is for actual economic mobility. It seems to me like banks do it because profit trumps the greater good of humanity.

As this parallel world of the super rich flourishes, the exorbitant disparity between the financial top and bottom is increasing. According to many economic indicators, this disparity will only sharpen, and economic policy will continue to spearhead this divide. In the past 10 minutes alone, while you were reading this book, the 10 of the richest people in the world earned more than $80 million, which is more than what the majority of people will earn in 10 lifetimes! This is unsustainable for the long term, and can lead to an oligarchy society if it continues at this pace. Financial education is key to equalizing this social-economic dilemma.

Money is a TOOL, not GOD

With all of the talk throughout this book pointing to money as a way to combat financial and societal problems, you're probably thinking that I consider money as the end-all be-all. As if money is the boarding pass needed to banish yourself from societal perils, and is the only way out of psychological warfare. I don't think so. What I am simply saying is that if you are in a game, which we all are, you must learn the rules, functions, and traps in order to excel at this game of money. The financial game that we play is the game of "who is indebted to whom?" This simple question determines who has the access to power needed for financial freedom, and who is financially dependent upon the mercy of the financial rulers who are the debtors. The game's outcomes reach far beyond the realm of our current reality, but affect our everyday life to the lives that have yet been thought of—our future generations. It's unfortunate that we have two sides of the economic societal table; one playing in order to survive and the other side playing as a way of keeping score. Money is simply a ledger; a by-product of manufactured success and social Darwinism, almost as though it were a measuring stick to see who is bigger. If money is the culprit, then primal competition is its accomplice.

Money has been used since the dawn of the shift from Neanderthals to modern humanity. In a way, money—whether it be in the form of cattle, a scarce natural resource, seashells, paper, or digital ones and zeros in cyberspace—has always been the primary, real innovative technology. It enhanced society in a way that rivals both the industrial and digital age, allowing for exponential growth and organized civilization. We can argue the adverse effects of it. However, I look at money like I do fire or a gun; it is only dangerous in the hands of dangerous people. Hopefully, in my lifetime, the future of money will conceive a checks and balances system, creating a new, true free market, relinquishing the players who seek to use it as a way to destroy, mislead, and manipulate the end user of money, and instead reward the people who reflect the good in the world.

Is there more?

A recording artist known as Drake brought up something interesting in one of his lyrics. As he reflected on his past experiences in relation to success and luxury, he said, "Is there more to life than digits and banking accounts?" He added, "Am I missing something that's more important to find, like healing my soul, like family time?" There are in fact things more than money, such as education, self-worth, honor, integrity, family, respect, and many other qualities that help make society better. I think people are afraid not of the money itself, but what money has become to society. We value, no worship, something that has been extracted from a tree. Almost like the forbidden apple, see the correlation? It wasn't the apple, but human nature that sparked evil. Money is simply a reflection of our actions. It's like fire; it can be used to do the most generous and fantastical things. Yet it can also be used for devastation, racism, scarcity, corruption, and many other unimaginable things. There is more to life than money; however, we must learn to understand it, if we want to understand people.

The real currency is YOU!

The currency in your pocket, or wallet, is simply a medium of exchange. It is a ledger; a medium of account because it has numbers on it. It is portable, which means you can take it wherever you go, and fungible, which means it works anywhere with either the same, or equivalent, amount. All of the ingredients for a revolutionary innovation that everyone can support and use. Seems like the best invention ever; almost too good to be true, right? Well, there is only one problem with currency. Because governments and banks can print more and more of it, dilute and control the supply, over time the value of this currency can rot away faster than an apple in a tree.

Welcome to the twilight zone! It is a universal fact that every single time a currency backed by a promise is introduced, it has always failed. It has a 100% failure rate. But there is one thing that will never fail. One thing that will never stop innovating, thinking, creating, or building; that is YOU. The currency represents your blood, your sweat, your time, your ideas, and your sacrifice. You, my friend, are what gives any currency its value. The real value of anything in life lies within knowledge and information. Your knowledge is and will always be the currency.

> *The definition of power is freedom, when*
> *you have power, you are free.*
>
> —Nasir Jones

10 things you will learn from reading my books

How to *sell*

How to *think freely*

How to *negotiate*

How to *respond to failure*

How to *invest money*

Principles of *success*

How to *handle money*

How to *make an impact*

How to *start a business*

How to *read any financial statement*

BONUS!

7 Steps to Financial Freedom

Want to be financially free?

The true goal of financial freedom is not to make enough money to buy any object that you want. Instead, the goal of financial freedom is to make money *NEVER* be an object! It's a subtle, but huge difference. If pursuing multiple streams of income, acquiring assets that pay you, being your own boss, or even having the freedom to make your own schedule sounds daunting and unrealistic to you, then you must simply alter your way of thinking. Ultimately, if you are interested in pursuing financial freedom, you must first change your mind-set. Let's take a look at the seven steps to achieving financial freedom:

1. Don't just save to save — Save to invest

Most people will advise you to simply "save your money" in order to build wealth. However, money is no longer money after 1971. So today, when bonds are paying almost zero and the Federal Reserve is printing trillions of dollars in fiat currency, pitching "saving money" is terrible advice. Since our government can mandate the amount of money that can be printed, every dollar you save becomes subjected to government control. As more money is printed, your dollar decreases in purchasing power and the money you have in the bank becomes worthless over time. As the dollar loses value every time more money is printed, saving is a sure way to let the government and banks take your money through inflation and taxes.

Unfortunately, many of us are still only saving, and it is now the worst time to save. This constant cognitive reinforcement while expecting different results can be considered a form of insanity. Instead, using it to buy assets that pay you positive cash flow can increase your wealth. Remember, a true investor and a financially educated person can make money when the economy is up and can make even more money in a bad economy.

2. Ignore 'thy' ignorance about money

To actually understand the language of money and how to stay ahead of the curve, you must ignore your ignorance about money and retrain your mind to see the other side of the coin. If you are part of the 99% of the population that has to share less than 40% of the wealth generated within our economy, then everything you have been taught about money is keeping you from reaching financial freedom. The information that is currently being spread through-out the masses tells us that "debt is bad," that we should "work for money," or that we should "focus on saving or paying down debt." However, this advice will only keep you in the rat race and dependent on the government. Breaking free of these invisible chains and financial dependence will require more than just having a salary, pension, and 401k. You will need to understand how you can use the liquidity you have to buy assets that appreciate and pay you while you wait. The truth is we all can make money, but only a few of us can reach financial freedom and wealth. Arriving at this plateau takes not only knowledge but a burning desire to become free from economic deprivation and the ability to see and leverage both sides of the economic coin (income and debt).

3. Sell the eggs, not the goose!

Have you ever read the story of the goose that laid the golden eggs? This simple story applies to finance in so many ways. In our current economy, the people who get crushed are the people who invest for capital gains and not cash flow. It does not matter what market you are in. Whether it's stocks, commodities, real estate, or business, if you are going into it hoping to sell to a bigger idiot than you, you are playing the wrong game.

Let's look at a brief example of someone buying for capital gains:

- You buy something at $5 and hope to sell it later for $10. You purchase a house for $300,000 and hope to flip it for $600,000. You buy a penny stock for $0.05 and try to sell it for more.

These examples show people investing for capital gains. When I invest, I invest for cash flow. In my opinion, how I invest is a lot like the game Monopoly. It goes as follows:

- One green house gives me $50; two green houses give me $100. Three green houses give me $150, and then I do what is called a 1031 exchange and buy one red hotel that makes me $500 in cash flow.

It's not rocket science! You don't even need a high school diploma to understand this basic formula of wealth creation. I just keep buying assets, and they pay me a consistent monthly income. The more assets I accumulate, the more I make in monthly income. It is just that simple. Capital gains mean that hopefully there is someone stupid enough to relieve you of your stupidity. So if you're going to be smart, play the cash flow game. This will allow you to increase your wealth and get a positive income at the same time. Capital gains are like eating the goose instead of the golden eggs. It's foolish; why would you eat something that is producing golden eggs? Why would you eat the goose?

4. Bargain hunt like the rich

Many of us only shop for liabilities that are considered on sale, such as a nice car, exclusive sneakers, clothes, and jewelry. Although these items make us poorer and cost us money in the long run, we convince ourselves that this is the right way to bargain hunt and "save money." However, the wealthy approach to bargain shopping is completely different than that of the financially uneducated. The rich wait for pullbacks in the stock market and corrections in real estate and purchase these assets "on sale" as the herd begins to sell in fear. The rich also invest in assets such as businesses, gold and silver, and technologies that will be at the forefront in the future before people are made aware of it.

You must learn to see what the financially uneducated are blinded by and bargain hunt for assets rather than liabilities. Unfortunately, the poor mentality tells us to shop for liabilities that are on sale. Start to bargain hunt like the rich and learn to buy assets that are on sale. This is a proven way to increase your wealth and build your income stream so that you can buy liabilities on sale with the profits from your acquired assets. This technique is how you amass a real fortune within our society.

5. Frugality is freedom

Frugality is more about making distinctions between things that matter and things that don't matter than it is about saving money. Being frugal is a discipline that requires a strong sense of equanimity and EQ. It is also the closest thing to financial freedom. Once you make the connection between frugality and financial freedom, you are on your way to reaching millions. Frugality allows another friend of mine to get away with working less than eight hours a week. He makes $30 an hour, but he saves 40% of his income to invest, and the rest goes to living expenses—food, shelter, and water. This may sound like a nightmare until you hear that he is able to take three trips to exotic locations a year. Even better, the cash flow that he receives from his investments is funding these trips, and it only took him five years to set himself up like this financially.

6. Understand your number

Unfortunately, there are no guarantees that we will survive until the consensus retirement age or that the same rules of money (rates, regulations, and macroeconomics) will apply once we get to retirement. In order to achieve a financially free retirement, you must have a number in mind regarding the money you wish to accumulate as opposed to having an appropriate age range that you will retire at. This is because this fairy-tale notion of working and saving until you are 65 years of age ignores one rule of humanity: *we are all different and have different circumstances in life.* Having an "age cap" for retirement is like playing a game of musical chairs, and we know there always has to be one or two people standing at the end of that game. What if you are the one standing? This is why instead of having a cap for your age, you should set a number in mind that will allow you to live financially free. Doing this will not only make you stress-free as you begin to approach that age but will give you the discipline and clarity you need in order to reach your goal for retirement.

7. Fail fast

> *I have not failed. I've just found ten thou-*
> *sand ways that won't work.*
>
> —Thomas Edison

Do any of your fears consist of the following?

- Fear of failure

- Fear of rejection

- Fear of looking stupid

- Fear of messing up

- Fear of being wrong publicly

- Fear of being exposed

The longer it takes for you to embrace and get over your failures, the longer it will take for you to learn from them and achieve financial freedom. I recommend that if you must fail, you should fail fast and learn from your failures even quicker. Some failures may require more time to come back from than others, and others may even leave a bad taste in your mouth as you try to move forward from them. However, to move forward from these mishaps, I want you to ask yourself, "Did I die, or did I kill someone else?" If you did, then God bless you; I have nothing for you. However, if you didn't, lighten up! What didn't kill you (or anyone else) will only make you stronger and wiser. Embrace failure, because this is your inner compass; your inner divinity is checking in and putting you back on course to receive your true blessing. This is a blessing that no human engineering can ever take from you. This blessing is divine, and embracing failure is the key to unlocking this divinity. So don't be afraid of failure so much that you aren't willing to try and reach your true greatness. Understand that there is no security in life, only opportunity. Embrace it, learn from it, and move on! Because if you aren't moving, you might as well be dead.

MONEY IS NOT **EVIL**

It is actually a very powerful tool and arguably the most revolutionary product ever invented! Yes – Money is a form of technology.

Money is a store of our economic energy and a question of confidence. It can be used as a medium of exchange between each party.

Now the real question is, what is a form of money?

---

*Interest rates have been at the lowest historic numbers for the longest period of time in over **5,000** years!*

WEALTH STRATEGY BY AGE

20's — 3 mandates

Income – Producing multiple streams of it

*Asset accumulation – Acquisition of assets
that generate cash flow for you*

*Capital appreciation – Should always be the "icing
on the cake" on every asset you acquire*

30's — 3 mandates

*Asset accumulation – Ramp up, but keep volatility low (acqui-
sition of assets should be calculated at this period of your life)*

*Income – Focus on maximizing the incomes that are
most profitable (nurture them, buy either reinvesting,
retraining, refurbishing, updating, or cultivating)*

Preservation of wealth – Capital preservation, dividend, cash flow

40's, 50's, and beyond

Wealth preservation – Capital preservation, dividend, cash flow

*Asset & capital appreciation – It is imperative that
you keep volatility low (acquisition of assets should
be calculated at this period of your life)*

*Income – Income should come from multiple sources (pas-
sive, portfolio and ordinary/retirement income)*

"Legacy insurance" – *trust, life insurance, etc.* – *Focus on setting up trusts, wills, and life insurance for your loved ones*

AUTHOR'S MOTIVATION

Writing isn't about making money, getting famous, getting dates, or making friends. In the end, it's about enriching the lives of those who will read your work, and enriching your own life, as well. It's about getting up, getting well, and getting over.

ABOUT THE AUTHOR

Jeremiah J. Brown is a tech entrepreneur, product strategist, and bestselling author of the book titled *Financial Freedom: My Only Hope*. At 18, he became a real estate agent in his hometown of New York City. Before graduating with a degree in finance, he launched and sold his first company and mobile application.

In addition to being an entrepreneur, Brown owns various properties throughout the United States. He's invested in the stock market and experienced firsthand its many ups and downs. Over time, Brown has learned to be an effective leader and to build his wealth from the bottom up.

Even before the age of 30, he's already achieved success with multiple business ventures. He's also been featured in various publications, including *Ebony Magazine, Respect, Newsweek, Billboard,* and *Entrepreneur Magazine*. Brown's entrepreneurship has allowed him to become an investor—an investor in people, and in the education of those who desire to be financially free. Despite the obstacles, Brown has shown that it is possible to achieve financial freedom in spite of any setback.

REACH OUT!

@iamjeremiahb

iamjeremiahb

Jeremiah Brown

Money is about trust, and trust can fall apart.

—*Jeremiah Brown*

ACKNOWLEDGEMENTS

This time around I want to thank my readers. You have stuck with me throughout this entire process, absorbed every word, and you guys are now putting the knowledge receive into practice. I hope this book has given you more value than a traditional MBA education. Thank you for banking on yourselves! Thanks to my family AJ, Rich, Anne, Uncle Brandon, Angelica, Ronisa, Danny, Donna, Rhonda, Big Sid, Aunty, Amanda, John, Kainon, Larry Patterson, Aunt Monica, Uncle Rob, John Daniels, and Bob Wynn for all supporting me, whether physically or in spirit, through this process. Thank you to the two most beautiful and wonderful women in my life, Angela Vega and Sydney Brown. Angela, you've taught me since birth the value of seeing things through, even if the odds are stacked and I am forever grateful to you and your unconditional love. Sydney, from reading early drafts to giving me advice on the cover to keeping the motivation constant, you were as important to this book getting done as I was, and I thank God for bringing you into my life! To Kene, Kim, and the NFTE team for supporting me and allowing me to be an avid supporter and speaker for NFTE. Kene, your work has been a key component to the success of entrepreneurs all over, and is really changing the lives of young people. I am grateful to you all, and I truly hope to spearhead a new wave of financially enlightened and aware people, who will transcend even my existence and last for generations. This book is for you!

CPSIA information can be obtained
at www.ICGtesting.com
Printed in the USA
LVHW050732180723
752687LV00034B/1282/J